THE JEWISH WOMEN'S STUDIES GUIDE,
Second Edition-1987

Compiled by
Sue Levi Elwell

UNIVERSITY
PRESS OF
AMERICA

BIBLIO
PRESS

LANHAM • NEW YORK • LONDON

British Cataloging in Publication Information Available

Co-published by arrangement with Biblio Press, Fresh Meadows, N.Y.

Library of Congress Cataloging-in-Publication Data

The Jewish women's studies guide.

  Includes bibliographies.
    1. Women, Jewish—Study and teaching (Higher)—
United States. 2. Women, Jewish—Study and teaching
(Continuing education)—United States. 3. Women in
Judaism—Study and teaching (Higher)—United States.
4. Women in Judaism—Study and teaching (Continuing
education)—United States. 5. Women, Jewish—
Bibliography. 6. Women in Judaism—Bibliography.
I. Elwell, Ellen Sue Levi.
HQ1172.J49   1987   016.3054'862   87-10836
ISBN 0-8191-6412-7 (alk. paper)
ISBN 0-8191-6413-5 (pbk. : alk. paper)

For further information about two out-of-print titles mentioned
frequently in this work, *The Jewish Women's Studies Guide* 1982
first edition, and *The Jewish Woman Bibliography*, 1900-1980
(1979, etc.), please contact the publisher,
Biblio Press, Fresh Meadows, N.Y. 11365-0022

TABLE OF CONTENTS

C. **Adult and Continuing Education Courses**

Introduction

Mother, asks the clever daughter,
Who our mothers?
Who are our ancestors?
What is our history?
Give us our name.
Name our geneology.

from **A Woman's Haggadah**
E. Broner and N. Nimrod

JEWISH WOMEN'S STUDIES is part of a very exciting revolution in the history of Jewish thought. After centuries of silence, Jewish women's stories are being woven into the rich tapestry that is the written heritage of the Jewish people. New research in Jewish women's history, Jewish women's writings, and Jewish women's spiritual and religious lives has begun to fill the void left by centuries of scholarship that concentrated solely on the historical, literary, and religious achievements of Jewish men. For the first time, the saga of the wanderings of the Jewish people: geographical, philosophical, psychological and spiritual, includes a full complement of Jewish voices; women's songs are finally being added to the repertoire.

But Jewish women's studies is much more than just another new field of academic inquiry. Courses in Jewish women's studies stretch our understanding of the nature of academic inquiry itself. Courses in Jewish women's studies challenge long-held stereotypes not only of Jews and of women but of the "insider" and the "outsider," and lead us to reexamine how such categories affect our lives. Such courses challenge our perception of ourselves, as individuals and as members of various communities. Such courses inspire as well as instruct, and often lead both learners and instructors beyond the classroom into the synagogue, the federation boardroom, and into the community with a new sense of the power of Jewish women's past and the potential of Jewish women's future.

In the four years since Edward Levenson and I compiled the first edition of the **Jewish Women's Studies Guide**, courses that either focus on or integrate the study of Jewish women have been developed and taught at many public and private colleges and universities across the country. Such courses are among the offerings of departments of History, Religious Studies, Jewish Studies, Sociology, Literature, and Women's Studies. Increasing numbers of synagogues and Jewish community centers feature such courses among their offerings, and many annual conferences and yearly programs for National Women's History Month in March now include sessions on Jewish women's history, culture, spirituality, and creative expression. The National Women's Studies Association now includes a Jewish Women's Caucus, which sponsors sessions, panels and workshops at yearly conventions.

The first edition of this **Guide** included 15 syllabi: 8 university courses on Jewish women, 2 courses that integrated Jewish women's studies into the university curriculum, and 5 courses designed particularly for adult and continuing education courses in non-university settings. The course syllabi in this updated collection reflect the increasing acceptance of such courses in all quarters. In addition, these new syllabi reflect the increased degree of specialization made possible by the swelling number of resources available. Especially notable are the five syllabi that integrate Jewish Women's studies into other courses, four of which are new additions to the **Guide**. These courses have been taught by scholars in a range of institutions, including the Jewish Theological Seminary ("Jewish Family in History and Literature") and the State University of New York at Buffalo ("American Jewish Experience"). While the number of courses in the category of Adult and Continuing Education remains the same as in the first edition, the content reflects the increasing sophistication and specialization within the field. Irene Fine's ground-breaking "Creating Midrash" course (Women's Institute for Continuing Jewish Education, San Diego) has been adapted by teachers and study groups across the country as women have reclaimed this ancient exegetical skill. Sharon Kleinbaum's course, "World of our Mothers: Jewish Women and Yiddish Literature" poses new questions to the rich world of Yiddish Literature.

The syllabi presented in this second edition of the **Guide** mirror the increased number of approaches now available. Many new books have appeared that have deepened our understanding and have suggested additional areas of inquiry. Some recent additions to the growing body of works in the field of Jewish women's studies are Evelyn Beck's ground-breaking **Nice Jewish Girls: A Lesbian Anthology**, originally issued by Persephone Press and now published by The Crossing Press; Julie R. Spitzer's **Rabbinic Attitudes on Spouse Abuse**, published by the National Federation of Temple Sisterhoods, and **The Tribe of Dina**, a rich anthology that was originally published as a special edition of **Sinister Wisdom**. Marcia Falk's article on creating new liturgy in the March 1985 issue of **Moment**, "What About God?" and Martha Ackelsberg's "Spirituality, Community, and Politics: **B'not Esh** and the Feminist Reconstruction of Judaism" in the Spring, 1986 **Journal of Feminist Studies in Religion** address the challenge of feminism to traditional Jewish religious life and religious communities. Penina V. Adelman's **Miriam's Well: Rituals for Jewish Women Around the Year** (Biblio Press, 1986) introduces the rich world of women's ritual. T. Drorah Setel's bold "Feminist Insights and the Question of Method" in Adela Yarbro Collins' **Feminist Perspectives on Biblical Scholarship** and her "Prophets and Pornography: Female Sexual Imagery in Hosea" in Letty Russell's **Feminist Interpretation of the Bible** offer fascinating new interpretations of Biblical texts. Ellen Umansky's **Lily Montague and the Advancement of Liberal Judaism: From Vision to Vocation** poses questions about one woman's choice of a religious vocation and challenges traditional interpretations of contemporary Jewish history. Judith Plaskow's "Standing Again at Sinai: Jewish Memory from a Feminist Perspective" in **Tikkun** I:2 is an incisive contribution to the development of a Jewish feminist theology.

Many of these new resources -- and other new works -- are included on the reading lists of the syllabi presented here. But as new scholarship appears, the task of integrating it into continuing courses remains. While many topics are addressed by the syllabi which follow, there are other areas of inquiry still to be developed. For example, there is no course on Israeli women. Also lacking is a course on the experience and writings of Sephardic women. Many have asked if it is possible to transcend the androcentric bias of Jewish mysticism and to develop a balanced course on women in/and Jewish mysticism. We are also missing courses on Jewish women in the plastic arts, and on Jewish women's contributions to the world of music as composers, conductors, and performers of vocal and instrumental music. All who use this **Guide** are encouraged to develop such courses, so that subsequent editions will be even more comprehensive.

Many thanks to the teachers and scholars across the country who submitted syllabi for inclusion in this **Guide**. This **Guide** could not have been published without their patience and cooperation.

This collection is dedicated to the teachers and students who are finding their mothers, meeting their ancestors, claiming their history, speaking their names and naming their geneology. Together, we will make the story of Judaism and the Jewish people complete.

Sue Levi Elwell
Los Angeles, 1987

JEWISH WOMEN WRITERS: AUTOBIOGRAPHY AND MEMOIR, FICTION, POETRY AND ESSAY

Evelyn Torton Beck
University of Maryland

"Jewish Women Writers: Autobiography and Memoir, Fiction, Poetry and Essay," represents a unique contribution to this collection, and is an updated version of Beck's course included in the first edition of the Guide. Evelyn Beck's annotated bibliography can serve as the outline for a complete course, or selections from the outline can be integrated into university or community courses on Jewish women. Beck's sensitivity to the wide range of Jewish women's voices renders her comments particularly useful, and she enables both experienced teachers and those teaching this material for the first time to make informed choices about the best selections for any audience. The works she discusses are arranged as follows:

I.   AUTOBIOGRAPHICAL WRITINGS AND MEMOIRS
          A.   By Individual Women Writers
          B.   Collective Works and Anthologies
II. FICTION
          A.   Novels
          B.   Short Story Collections
III. POETRY
          A.   Anthologies
          B.   Individual Poets
IV. FILMS
V.   THE VISUAL ARTS
VI. DRAMA
VII. TAPES

* * *

Course Description:

A brief glance at a typical college catalogue makes plain the bias of curriculum designers and reveals a focus on white, middle class, Christian males. In attempting to correct this imbalance, the recently established fields of Jewish Studies and Women's Studies have not always been careful to give sufficient attention to each other. In order to assure that higher education represents the diversity of our society, it is as essential to integrate material on Jewish women (in all of our diversity) into Jewish

1

Studies, as it is to include Jewish women in Women's Studies. Lesbian material should be included in both these areas.

The concept of inclusion is an ever-expanding category. The more one opens oneself to the idea that Jews are not a monolithic people, but represent a genuine diversity that often appears to, but need not threaten community, the more diversity one actually "sees." For example, it is only in the last two years that I have come to understand the importance of including Jews who have converted to Judaism as part of this diversity, because the convert's experiences are different from that of a "born Jew." This expanding consciousness is part of a continuing process. I am also increasingly aware of a distinct Ashkenazi bias in my choice of texts, which is not an evaluative statement, but the result of my previous training and experience. I am in the process of educating myself as quickly as I can. The essays by Arditti and Wachs in The Tribe of Dina (see B 1.) are especially helpful in providing information and bibliography on Sephardi Jews.

The syllabus that follows brings together those works of Jewish women writers that I have previously (and successfully) included in a variety of courses such as Yiddish Literature in Translation, Comparative Literature, Women in Arts, Minority Women in the Arts, Women Writers, Feminist Criticism, Autobiography, and Lesbian Culture. This syllabus may be used as it stands (pruned to fit the time frame of a single semester) or, selections from it may be integrated into courses whose primary focus is elsewhere--the novel and short story, autobiography, poetry, drama, working class literature, Jewish women. These writers represent a variety of class backgrounds, ages, geographical settings, languages, sexual orientations and life choices, including the degree of adherence to traditional Jewish religious practices. Many would define themselves as Jewish atheists. All, however, write as women and/or lesbians conscious of their Jewish identities. Most are of Ashkenazi backgrounds, and, unless otherwise indicated, write in English. Almost all the books listed are currently in print and available in paperback editions. Readers should however be warned that these texts go in and out of print (and change publishers) with alarming regularity. In all sections, texts are arranged chronologically (in order of writing, not according to date of publication).

I.   AUTOBIOGRAPHICAL WRITINGS AND MEMOIRS

A.   By Individual Women Writers

1.   Gluckel. The Memoirs of Gluckel of
     Hameln   (1646-1724).   Marvin
     Lowenthal, Trans.   NY: Schocken
     Books, 1977.
     Written in 1690, first published in
     English in 1932, and reprinted in 1977,
     these are the memoirs of a powerful
     Jewish woman who bore thirteen children.
     After her first husband's death, Gluckel
     ran his business single-handedly.
     Includes much social history and a good
     account of what it was like to be a
     Jewish woman in seventeenth century
     Germany. (Translated from Yiddish.)

2.   Chagall, Bella. Burning Lights. NY:
     Schocken, 1962.
     Written in 1940, this is the memoir of a
     Russian girlhood that reflects the
     yearly holiday rituals that organize
     Jewish life. By the wife of the painter
     Marc Chagall. (Translated from
     Yiddish.)

3.   Antin, Mary. The Promised Land. NY:
     Houghton Mifflin, 1969.
     Written in 1912, this autobiography
     presents the story of an immigrant child
     from the shtetl assimilating into the
     American way of life in Boston, ending
     with her going to Columbia University.
     Antin believes in the promise of
     America and harshly exposes the sexism
     that she sees inherent in Orthodox
     Jewish practice and belief.

4.   Antin, Mary. From Plotzk to Boston.
     NY: Markus Wiener Publishing,
     1985.
     Written when Antin was 13 years old. Is
     considerably shorter and has a different
     tone than Promised Land, in its greater
     focus on the child's perspective and its
     more intense focus on the transition of
     immigration.

5. Yezierska, Anzia. <u>Red Ribbon on a White Horse</u>. 1950; rpt. NY: Persea Books, 1978.
    The autobiography of a most unusual life, by the author of <u>Bread Givers</u>. This story records Yezierska's rise from poverty to success in writing for Hollywood where she could not bear to be making a profit from the stories of her own people's sufferings. Because Yezierska was so burdened with guilt and unable to deal with the contradictions of Hollywood, her creativity dried up and she left this lucrative business.

6. Rosen, Ruth and Sue Davidson, eds. <u>The Mamie Papers</u>. Old Westbury, NY: Feminist Press in cooperation with the Schlesinger Library of Radcliffe College, 1977.
    These letters, written from 1910 to 1922, tell the story of one Jewish woman's struggle for survival. Mamie Pinzer works against a life of poverty, prostitution, and drug addiction. With the help of a non-Jewish woman of substantial means, Pinzer begins a career in business and eventually establishes her own mission house for "wayward" girls. The letters to her benefactor document her gradual development into a strong and dignified woman.

7. Trupin, Sophie. <u>Dakota Diaspora: Memoirs of a Jewish Homesteader</u>. Berkeley, CA: Alternative Press, 1984.
    The memoirs of a Jewish immigrant whose family settled on the plains of North Dakota. Trupin provides insight into a harsh living environment we rarely associate with Jews.

8. Simon, Kate. <u>Bronx Primitive: Portraits in a Childhood</u>. NY: Viking Press, 1982. Also available in paperback by Harper and Row.

4

9.   Simon, Kate. <u>A Wider World: Portraits
        in an Adolescence</u>. NY: Harper and
        Row, 1976. Hardback.
Wonderfully poignant, yet unsentimental
stories of growing up in New York City,
coming of age after WWI; funny and
tragi-comic autobiographical revelations
told with strong feminist understanding.
Simon's adventures are diverse and
unexpected from a Jewish women of her
time. Helps to break stereotypical
ideas of the "nice Jewish girl."

10.   Moskowitz, Faye. <u>A Leak in the Heart:
        Tales from a Woman's Life</u>. Boston:
        David R. Godine, 1985. (hardback
        only)
A   delightful first collection of
stories--autobiographical sketches with
philosophical underpinnings. They span
the author's life from childhood in the
Detroit Jewish ghetto and a small
Michigan town in which Jews were an
anomaly, to Washington, D.C. Documents
the lives of women in four generations.
"A Leak in the Heart" is her mother's
name for the illness that killed her
sister, but it becomes a metaphor for
many other leakages, such as languages,
tears, layers of time, even menstrual
blood. If it were available in
paperback I would recommend it strongly
for classroom use. I do so anyway.

11.   Chernin, Kim. <u>In My Mother's House: A
        Daughter's Story</u>. New Haven/New
        York: Ticknor and Fields, 1983
        (also in paper).
Chernin tells the story of her mother, a
Russian Jewish immigrant and a political
activist who was arrested and imprisoned
during the McCarthy era. In retelling
her mother's story she also tells her
own, a story of "conflict, confrontation
and reconciliation," a book about
"love, politics, forgiveness."

12. Jordan, Ruth. <u>Daughter of the Waves:
    Memoirs of Growing Up in Pre-War
    Palestine</u>. NY: Taplinger
    Publishing Co., 1983.
    This book documents not only the memoirs
    of a childhood, but life in Palestine
    under the British mandate, and the
    intense cultural, intellectual and
    political struggles of the period.

13. Hazelton, Leslie. <u>Jerusalem, Oh
    Jerusalem</u>. New York, 1986.
    Personal/political memoirs, descrip-
    tions, analyses by the author of <u>The
    Israeli Woman: Myths and Realities</u>.
    Having left Israel, after having made
    <u>aliya</u> thirteen years before, she
    returns, only to find she cannot stay
    away despite the pain of the current
    political situation there and the
    pressures on women.

14. Stern, Elisabeth, G. (pseud. Leah
    Morton). <u>I Am a Woman--and a Jew</u>.
    NY: Arno Press and the N.Y. Times,
    1969.
    This 1969 reprint of a 1926 book is
    extremely fascinating as the daughter of
    an Orthodox Jewish man (the father looms
    large) struggles with the divisions
    within herself: the denials, the
    attempts to embrace her Jewish self. In
    many ways, a very modern text.

# # #

Because of the emergence of so many Holocaust memoirs
by women, I am treating these texts somewhat
differently, and annotating only some of these texts.
It seems important to keep a record of as many of these
texts by women as possible, since history has shown us
that women's voices are easily lost.

15. Frank, Anne. <u>The Diary of a Young Girl</u>.
    1952; rpt. NY: Doubleday, 1967.
    Diary of a young girl hiding from the
    Nazis in occupied Holland. Records her
    coming to young womanhood and her
    observations of what it means to be

Jewish and in danger of your life for
that reason alone. (Translated from
Dutch.)

16. Hillesum, Etty. An Interrupted Life:
    The Diaries of Etty Hillesum. NY:
    Pantheon Books, 1983. (also in
    paper)
    The intimate journal of a young Jewish
    woman born into a privileged and highly
    assimilated Dutch family. This journal
    describes her inner life in the war
    years 1941-43 when she is living in
    Amsterdam; the diary ends abruptly when
    she is deported to Auschwitz in
    September 1943, where she died at the
    age of 29.

17. Fenelon, Fania. Playing for Time. NY:
    Berkeley Publishing Co., 1977.
    Memoir of a Paris cabaret singer and a
    secret member of the Resistance who was
    captured by the Nazis. Fenelon survived
    Auschwitz as a member of an all women's
    orchestra whose members were allowed to
    live only as long as they continued to
    make music for the Germans. (Translated
    from French.)

18. Yago-Jung, Yudit. "Growing Up in
    Germany: After the War, After
    Hitler, Afterwards." New German
    Critique, 20 (Spring/Summer 1980),
    71-80. (Special Issue on Germans
    and Jews, No. II.)
    Describes the experience of growing up
    as a Jew in a virtually Jew-less Germany
    after the Second World War, culminating
    in Yago-Jung's decision to emigrate.

19. Jackson, Livia E. Bitton. Elli: Coming
    of Age in the Holocaust.
    Quadrangle: A Times Book, 1980.
    The story of a Hungarian girl who
    survives Auschwitz.

20. Leitner, Isabella. Fragments of
    Isabella: A Memoir of Auschwitz.
    NY: Thomas Y. Crowell, 1978. Also
    in paper, sequel also available.

7

21. Delbo, Charlotte. _None of us Will Return_. Boston: Beacon Press, 1968.
Powerfully understated, almost like a prose poem.

22. Tillion, Germaine. _Ravensbruck: Eyewitness Account of a Woman's Concentration Camp_. NY: Anchor Books, 1975.
One of the earliest women's eyewitness accounts.

23. Markish, Esther. _The Long Return_. NY: Ballantine, 1978.

24. Zyskind, Sara. _Stolen Years: A Child Survives Auschwitz_. NY: New American Library, 1981.

25. Bloch, Alice. _Lifetime Guarantee: A Journey Through Loss and Survival_. Watertown, MA: Persephone Press, 1981.

This is not a Holocaust memoir, but its theme of the tragic death of a young Jewish girl makes it appropriate to list after the Holocaust memoirs where the questions of justice and "why" also emerge as themes. The answers, of course, are equally ineffable. The chronicle of a young woman faced with the impending death of a younger sister who has cancer. The work explores the intense bond between sisters against a background of Jewish family dynamics and the author's coming to terms with her own lesbian identity. Its power lies in its sometimes painful honesty and its understatement, combined with an often lyric prose style; it also includes letters and fragments left by the dying sister.

B.   Collective Works and Anthologies

1.   Kaye/Kantrowitz, Melanie and Irena
          Klepfisz. The Tribe of Dina: A
          Jewish Women's Anthology.   Sinister
          Wisdom Books (Box 1308, Montpelier,
          VT   05602).
      A wonderfully diverse, rich anthology
      that includes fiction, poetry, essays
      and art work by Jewish women from many
      different cultures and countries.

2.   Nice Jewish Girls: A Lesbian Anthology.
          Evelyn   Torton   Beck,   ed.
          Trumansburg,   NY   (14886):   The
          Crossing Press, 1982.
      The   collective   works   of   Jewish
      lesbians--Afro-Judaic,   Arabic,
      Ashkenazi,   Sephardic--affirm   Jewish
      identity   and   confront   anti-Semitism
      inside and outside the women's movement.
      Poetry,   short   stories,   essays   and
      photographs.   Bibliography   includes   a
      section   on   "Jewish   Women/Women   of
      Color."

3.   Kramer, Sydelle and Jenny Masur.   Jewish
          Grandmothers.   Boston: Beacon
          Press, 1976.
      Ten Jewish grandmothers talk about their
      lives. All are immigrants from Eastern
      Europe who came to the United States in
      the   early   years   of   the   twentieth
      century.   They   describe   their
      experiences   of   pogroms,   the   Great
      Depression,   poverty,   and   the   culture
      shock they experienced; many   outlived
      their husbands and survived alone for
      many years. With photographs.

4.   Metzger, Isaac, ed. A Bintel Brief, 2
          vols.   Vol. 1:   1906-1967.   NY:
          Ballantine Books, 1971; Vol.   2:
          1950-1980. NY: Viking, 1981.
      These letters from readers of the Jewish
      Daily Forward reveal the shifts as well
      as the continuity of problems that have
      plagued Jewish immigrants to the United
      States from the turn of the century to
      the present. Many of the letter writers

are women seeking advice about the difficulties in rearing their Jewish children, surviving when husbands abandon them, as well as dealing with parents who continue to demand much of their adult children.

5. Myerhoff, Barbara. <u>Number Our Days</u>. NY: Dutton, 1978.
A Jewish anthropologist documents Jews living in difficult circumstances--in poverty, and on the margins of society, in a neighborhood that was once Jewish and has become run-down and inhospitable to them. Set in Southern California. These open and candid interviews have been made into a wonderful film of the same name.

6. Morales, Aurora Levins and Rosario Morales. <u>Getting Home Alive</u>. Ithaca, NY (14850): Firebrand Books (141 The Commons, Ithaca).
In a variety of forms--defying genre categorization--this mother and daughter circle the questions: What does it mean to be a Puerto Rican Jewish American? What does it mean to be dark-skinned, Jewish and Latina?

7, Rabinowitz, Dorothy. <u>New Lives</u>. NY: Avon, 1977.
Interviews with survivors of the Holocaust living in the United States.

8. Epstein, Helen. <u>Children of the Holocaust: Conversations with Sons and Daughters of Survivors</u>. NY: Bantam, 1980.
Interviews with children of Holocaust survivors in the United States, Canada, and Israel.

9. Steinitz, Lucy Y. with D. Szonyi. <u>Living After the Holocaust: Reflections by Children of Survivors in America</u>. NY: Bloch Publishers, 1975.

10

10. Moskowitz, Sarah. <u>Love Despite Hate:</u>
<u>Child Survivors of the Holocaust</u>
<u>and their Adult Lives.</u> NY:
Schocken, 1983. (with
illustrations) Hardback

11. Vegh, Claudine. <u>I Didn't Say Goodbye:</u>
<u>Interviews with Children of the</u>
<u>Holocaust.</u> NY: E.P. Dutton, 1984.

12. Laska, Vera. <u>Women in the Resistance</u>
<u>and the Holocaust: The Voices of</u>
<u>Eyewitnesses.</u> Conn: Greenwood
Press, 1983.

13. <u>Anthology of Holocaust Literature</u>, Jacob
Glatstein, ed. NY: Atheneum
Press, 1972.
At least half the entries are by women.
Excellent variety of selections in a
number of genres, translated from
Polish, Russian, German, Italian,
Hebrew, and Yiddish.

II. FICTION

A. Novels

1. Yezierska, Anzia. <u>Bread Givers.</u> NY:
Persea Books, 1975.
This 1925 novel portrays a young
immigrant's growing up in New York City
in a family where the father rules
supreme and poverty is a determining
factor. Against these pressures, the
narrator determines to "make something
of herself" and successfully works her
way through college by taking on a
variety of exhausting and spiritually
demoralizing jobs. The language is a
wonderful recreation of Yiddish.

2. Kreitman, Esther. <u>Deborah.</u> Great
Britain: Virago Press, 1983.
An autobiographical novel, depicting the
double oppression of life in the shtetl
for a Jewish woman. Kreitman is the
sister of the brothers Singer and may
have begun to write before they did.
This book was first published in Yiddish

11

in 1936 and translated by her son in
1946. "This is a woman's voice that has
never been heard before--from the
depths of the ghetto of Jewish women."

3. Broner, E.M. Her Mothers. NY:
    Berkeley Publishing Company, 1975.
The story of a Jewish mother seeking her
daughter and her mother--and mothers.

_____. A Weave of Women. NY:
    Bantam Books, 1962.
The interweaving of the lives of a
spectrum of women who converge in
Israel: Jewish and non-Jewish; Arab,
European, Israeli and American.

4. Schaeffer, Susan Fromberg. Anya. NY:
    Avon Books, 1976.
The story of a young, wealthy Jewish
woman whose life is irrevocably altered
by the Holocaust. From being a
privileged medical student in Warsaw,
she finds herself in a concentration
camp. The book chronicles her survival
and emigration to America.

5. Nachman, Elana. Riverfinger Women.
    Plainfield, VT: Daughters Press,
    1974.
This novel, through the powerful voice
of Inez Riverfinger, portrays what it
was like to be a young Jewish lesbian in
the late 60s in the United States. It
is a journey through time and space,
through politics and the personal.
Funny as well as serious.

6. Toder, Nancy. Choices. Watertown, MA:
    Persephone Press, 1980.
A novel about a Jewish lesbian's life
through college and into the
professional world.

7. Geller, Ruth. Triangles. Trumansburg,
    NY: The Crossing Press, 1984.
The story of a Jewish lesbian's coming
to consciousness as a lesbian and as a
Jew who begins to understand the
interconnectedness of anti-Semitism,

12

racism, homophobia and class bias, in herself and in the context of her family, especially the loving relationship with her grandmother and her non-Jewish lover.

8. Bloch, Alice. <u>The Law of Return</u>.
    Alyson Press, 1984.
    A novel about a young Jewish woman whose odyssey in search of the meaning of being Jewish and a woman take her to Israel where she meets a wide spectrum of people living there. Years later, she comes out as a lesbian but discovers the ironies in the "law of return" which explicitly excludes lesbians and gay Jews from claiming the right of citizenship in Israel.

9. Sinclair, Jo (pseud. of Ruth Seid). <u>The Changelings</u>. NY: The Feminist Press, 1985.
    This text, written in the fifties and dealing with the changing neighborhood in an Ohio city, in which Blacks are moving into a previously working class white Jewish neighborhood. Because of the friendship that forms between two adolescent girls, one Christian and Black, one Jewish, this text has become very popular in Women's Studies courses and is held up as an example of what is possible between different ethnic and religious groups. I find the text exceedingly problematic, because it presents an entirely one-sided, negative view of Jewish racism and makes no mention of Jewish activism <u>against</u> racism, which is also historically more accurate. The Feminist Press was exceedingly remiss in commissioning two Afterwords by Black women and not allowing any Jewish women to have a voice. The friendship of the two young girls in the book does not mitigate the distorted portrait of Jews who seem to have no purpose in life but the fear and hatred of Blacks. This gross exaggeration also makes for bad writing.

10. Segal, Lore. Her First American. NY: Alfred A. Knopf, 1985.
A Viennese born girl who has spent her life running from Hitler comes to the United States in search of her mother and begins the process of fitting into American life.

11. Kerr, Judith. When Hitler Stole Pink Rabbit. NY: Dell, 1971.
For young adults. Story of a German Jewish family's flight from Hitler's Germany. Told from the child's point of view, it depicts life as it was experienced by some refugees, in this case, life in Switzerland.

B. Short Story Collections

1. Olsen, Tillie. Tell Me a Riddle. NY: Dell, 1968.
The title story of this collection tells the story of a dying old Jewish woman in a love/hate struggle with her husband of forty-seven years. The novella is tightly compressed--a gem evoking time past and present, Yiddish in English, the tragic and the comic.

2. Yezierska, Anzia. The Open Cage: An Anzia Yezierska Collection. NY: Persea Books, 1979.
This book contains stories written between the 1920s and 1964, and it offers vivid portrayals of one woman's view of Jewish life in America during those years.

3. _____. Hungry Hearts and Other Stories. NY: Persea Books, 1985.

4. Paley, Grace. The Little Disturbances of Man. NY: Penguin Books, 1985.

5. _____. Enormous Changes at the Last Minute. NY: Farrar, Straus & Giroux, 1974.

6. _____. Later the Same Day.
NY: Farrar, Straus & Giroux, 1985.
Paley's stories are quintessentially New
York Jewish. They bring together the
ethnicity of the city---in all its
diversity--while focusing on the lives
of people who all too often remain
invisible.

7. Ozick, Cynthia. "The Pagan Rabbi" and
Other Stories. NY: Schocken,
1976.
Ozick writes more in the tradition of
certain Jewish male writers--Bellow,
Malamud, and Isaac Bashevis Singer, than
in the tradition of feminist Grace
Paley. Ozick's writing is powerful but
does not further our search for
understanding the lives of Jewish women.
Ozick's feminist viewpoint (often
articulated in her essays) is not at
work in her fiction.

8. Mazow, Julia Wolf. The Woman Who Lost
Her Names: Selected Writings by
Jewish American Women. San
Francisco: Harper and Row, 1981.
This collection includes the work of
some women whose writings are relatively
little known. It also includes two
lesbian selections, one by Elana Nachman
(from Riverfinger Women), the other by
Thyme Seagull, "My Mother was a Light
Housekeeper."

III. POETRY

A. Anthologies

1. The Other Voice: 20th Century Women's
Poetry in Translation, Joanna
Bankier, et al., eds. NY: W.W.
Norton, 1976.
From Hebrew: Leah Goldberg and Dahlia
Ravikovitch; from Yiddish: Kadia
Molodowsky, Anna Margolin, Celia
Dropkin, and Malka Heifetz Tussman; from
German: Else Lasker-Schuler.

2. The Penguin Book of Women Poets, Carol
        Cosman, et al., eds. NY: Penguin,
        1979.
    From Song of Songs; Sephardic Ballad
    (both anonymous). From Yiddish: Malka
    Heifetz Tussman, Kadia Molodowsky, and
    Rachel Korn; from Hebrew: Rahel, Leah
    Goldberg, and Dahlia Ravikovitch; from
    German: Gertrud Kolmar, Else Lasker-
    Schuler; in English: Muriel Rukeyser.
    (The selections in 1 and 2 above are not
    the same in the two volumes.)

3. A Treasury of Yiddish Poetry, Irving
        Howe and Eliezer Greenberg, eds.
        NY: Schocken, 1976.
    Poetry by Kadia Molodowsky, Rachel Korn,
    and others.

4. Burning Air and a Clear Mind:
        Contemporary Israeli Women Poets,
        Myra Glazer, ed. Athens, Ohio:
        Ohio University Press, 1981.

B. Individual Poets

1. Kolmar, Gertrud. Dark Soliloquy:
        Selected Poems of Gertrud Kolmar.
        Dual language edition (German/
        English). NY: Seabury Press,
        1975.
    Kolmar's images are powerfully female.
    She writes passionately as a Jewish
    woman, at a time when Hitler was coming
    to power in Germany. She died in
    Auschwitz at the age of 48.

2. Sachs, Nelly. O the Chimneys:
        Selected Poems, Including "Eli," A
        Verse Play. NY: Farrar, Straus,
        and Giroux, 1967.
    Translated from German.

3. Goldberg, Leah. Selected Poems of Leah
        Goldberg. London and San
        Francisco: Menard and Panjandrum
        Presses, 1976.
    Translated from Hebrew.

16

4. Parnok, Sophia. "8 Poems." in
    Conditions: Six,   1980,   pp.
    177-193.
    Woman-identified poet, lived openly in
    Russia as a lesbian. Translated from
    Russian by Rima Shore.

5. Klepfisz, Irena. Keeper of Accounts.
    Persephone Press, 1982, distributed
    by Sinister Wisdom Books, Box 1308,
    Montpelier, VT 05602.
    This is the powerful voice of a
    Holocaust survivor, a lesbian, an office
    worker, a poet struggling to survive
    and to create. Her poetry reflects the
    complexity of Jewish history, of being a
    woman and a Jew at a particular moment.
    The multi-leveled voices are rich and
    resonant.

6. _____ . Different Enclosures:
    Poetry and Prose. Great Britain:
    Onlywomen Press, 1985.
    Contains the entirety of an early book
    of Klepfisz poems, periods of stress;
    Keeper of Accounts; as well as the
    wonderfully imaged short story, "The
    Journal of Rachel Robotnick."

7. Kaye, Melanie. We Speak in Code: Poems
    & Other Writings. Pittsburgh, PA:
    Motherroot Publications, 1980.
    Powerfully feminist and Jewish, this
    book deals with growing up Jewish in
    Brooklyn, in a poor family still close
    to its immigrant roots. With visual
    art. (May be ordered from Sinister
    Wisdom Books.)

8. Shelley, Martha. Crossing the DMZ.
    Oakland, CA: Women's Press Collec-
    tive, 1974.

9. _____ . Lovers and Mothers.
    Oakland, CA: Sefir Publishing,
    1981.
    Strong collections of poems, the first
    dealing with the political issues of the
    1960s: the war in Vietnam, coming out
    as a lesbian, radical politics, being

Jewish. The second focuses on what it means when an American Jewish lesbian falls in love with an Israeli mother of three young children and they try to make a life together, struggling against chaos, inundation, and poverty. (Both may be ordered through Sefir Books, 542 25th Street, Apt. 335, Oakland, CA 94612.)

10. Rukeyser, Muriel. The Collected Poems of Muriel Rukeyser. NY: McGraw-Hill, 1979.
This collection concerns itself with racism, anti-Semitism, homophobia, and is fundamentally anti-war and sympathetic toward the small people whose lives are so often undocumented and uncelebrated. Only shortly before her death did Rukeyser openly identify as a lesbian.

11. Rich, Adrienne. Your Native Land, Your Life. NY: Norton, 1986.
Rich is increasingly focusing on her Jewish/lesbian identity and connecting her own personal history ("Split at the Root," see Nice Jewish Girls) with the history of the Jewish people, as well as that of other oppressed groups. This anthology contains the whole of the long poem "Sources" which deals with these very themes.

12. Pastan, Linda. PM/AM. NY: Norton, 1982.
That Pastan is a woman and a Jew is threaded throughout these poems, though Pastan does not identify herself as a Jewish woman poet.

IV. FILMS

1. Yudie. New Day Films. (See V. 4 for ordering details.)
The story of an immigrant woman who never marries and supports herself in New York City her entire life. Describes the joys of independence and the loneliness of old age. Filmed by Lynn Littman.

2. <u>Number Our Days</u>. Filmed by Lynn Littman.
    Based on the book of the same name (see
    I. B. 5).
    Distributed by Hackford/Littman, 6620
    Cahuenga Terrace, Los Angeles, CA 90068.
    (213) 467-6802.

3. <u>Julia</u>.
    Based on the story by Lillian Hellman.
    Described a young Jewish woman who chooses to
    do anti-Nazi work in Germany and is
    eventually killed in the process.

4. <u>They Are Their Own Gifts</u>. New Day Films,
    P.O. Box 315, Franklin Lakes, NY 07417.
    (201) 891-8240.
    Two of the three reels of this film about
    women artists concern Jewish women artists:
    Muriel Rukeyser, poet, and Anna Sokolow,
    choreographer. Interesting interweaving of
    documentation of their lives and past
    histories, with their artistic
    accomplishments and their understanding of
    themselves as artists. The three segments
    are available individually. Sokolow's Jewish
    identity is particularly clear in the dance
    "Dreams," a memorial to the Holocaust.

5. <u>Anu Banu: The Daughters of Utopia</u>. Order
    from Jewish Film Festival, 2600 10th
    Street, Room 102, Berkeley, CA 94210.
    (415) 548-0556.
    Interviews with early settlers.

6. <u>November Moon</u>.
    The story of two women who love each other,
    one Jewish, one not, who help each other
    survive the war.

V. THE VISUAL ARTS

1. Salomon, Charlotte. <u>Life or Theater: An
    Autobiographical Play</u>. NY: Viking
    Press, 1981.
    Paintings accompanied by words of the story
    of her life. Unique representation.
    Portraits in the vein of Expressionism;
    highly original perspective of the self in
    history. The artist did not survive the war.

19

2. Rubin, Gail. Psalmist with a Camera: Photographs of a Biblical Safari. NY: Abbeville Press, 1979.
    Incredible photos of wildlife in Israel, some female images that move toward the abstraction of an O'Keefe painting. The photographer was killed by terrorists while photographing.

3. Majaro-Mintz, Lea. Conversations in Clay. Jerusalem, Israel, 1980.
    Her clay figures of women are unique in portraying the many roles women take, and are a refreshing self-examination of feelings we have about being women.

4. Swartz, Beth Ames. Ten Sites Series. Slides available from Jewish Museum in New York City or Sandak, 180 Harvard Avenue, Stamford, CT 06902.
    The artist creates collages made on ten sites historically important to women in Israel. The work reflects the artist's concern with nature, ritual and history.

5. Wiseman, Adele. Old Women at Play. Toronto, Vancouver: Clarke, Irwin and Co., 1979.
    A Ukrainian Jewish woman makes hundreds of dolls from scraps. Pictures and interviews. This is the story of her art and life, recorded by her daughter.

VI. DRAMA

Delbo, Charlotte. "Who Will Carry the Word?" in Theater of the Holocaust, R. Skloot, ed. Madison, WI: University of Wisconsin Press, 1982.

VII. TAPES

1. "Feminist Jewish Women's Voices: Diversity and Community," a tape recording of a plenary made at the National Women's Studies Association Convention, University of Illinois, June 1986. Can be ordered from Caryn McTigue Musil, NWSA Coordinator, LaSalle University, Philadelphia, PA 10141, $6.50. Includes voices of Sephardic Jews, Jews who grew up in remote California

villages, Holocaust survivors, lesbians, and other experiences. Very powerful text.

2. "Jewish Lesbian Culture and Anti-Semitism in the Lesbian Community," a presentation by Minneapolis Jewish Lesbians. Available from Radical Rose Recordings, BDO 1, P.O. Box 8122, Minneapolis, MN 55408.

THE JEWISH WOMAN IN INTERNATIONAL PERSPECTIVE

Evelyn Torton Beck
University of Maryland

This course explores the diversity of Jewish women's experiences in the social, cultural, historical and religious contexts of Jewish life. Throughout, we will consider the impact of feminism on Judaism and the transformations Jewish woman are creating in contemporary Jewish thinking and in the Jewish institutions.

This course was offered in the Spring of 1986 as a special topics course in Women's Studies on the intermediate level and was cross-listed with the Jewish Studies Program. The course assumes some familiarity with feminist analyses and has the prerequisite of one introductory Women's Studies course. It would be possible to offer this as an introductory course if the teacher were willing to introduce students to feminist analyses at the same time that she is introducing them to the complexities of Jewish themes. I prefer to have some common ground at the start. I have been quite surprised to discover how little most non-Jewish students (and many Jewish students as well) know about Jewish history, customs, values and traditions.

REQUIRED TEXTS:

1. On Being a Jewish Feminist, Susannah Heschel, ed. NY: Schocken Press, 1983.

2. The Tribe of Dina: A Jewish Women's Anthology, Melanie Kaye/Kantrowitz and Irena Klepfisz, eds. Montepelier, VT: Sinister Wisdom Books, 1986. (Box 1308, Montepelier, VT 05602)

3. Nice Jewish Girls: A Lesbian Anthology, Evelyn Torton Beck, ed., Trumansburg, NY (14886): Crossing Press, rpt. 1984.

4. Deborah, Esther Kreitman, 1954, Great Britain: Virago Press, 1983.

5. Dakota Diaspora: Memoirs of a Jewish Homesteader, Alternative Press, 1984 (Box 4798, Berkeley, CA 94774).

6. <u>Bread Givers</u>, Anzia Yezierska, NY: Presea Press, 1975.

7. <u>Tell Me a Riddle</u>, Tillie Olsen, NY: Dell, 1968.

8. <u>A Weave of Women</u>, E.M. Broner, Boston: Beacon, 1978.

9. <u>Gluckl of Hameln</u>, NY: Schocken, 1977.

10. <u>Dona Gracia of the House of Nasi</u>, Cecil Roth, Philadelphia, PA: Jewish Publication Society of America, 1977.

11. <u>Keeper of Accounts</u>, Irena Klepfisz, Persephone Press, distributed by Sinister Wisdom, see 2 for address.

12. "Between Invisibility and Overvisibility: The Politics of Anti-Semitism in the Women's Movement and Beyond." Evelyn Torton Beck, <u>Working Papers in Women's Studies</u>, No. 11, University of Wisconsin Women's Studies Research Center, 209 North Brooks Street, Madison, WI 53715.

13. "Women Surviving the Holocaust: Conference Proceedings," Esther Katz and Joan Ringelheim, eds., Institute for Research in History, 432 Park Avenue, New York, NY 10016.

14. Films to be shown: <u>Yudie</u> (New Day Films, Box 315, Franklin Lakes, NJ 07417, (201) 891-8240).

    <u>Anu Banu: The Daughters of Utopia</u> (order from Jewish Film Festival, 2600 10th Street, Room 102, Berkeley, CA 94210 (415) 548-0556).

15. Slides: of works by Beth Ames Swartz (mixed media collages); Lea Majaro-Mintz (sculpture); Charlotte Saloman (watercolor), Gail Rubin (photography).

COURSE ASSIGNMENTS AND EXPECTATIONS:

1. Attendance at all classes and participation in discussion.

2.   Keep a weekly reading journal. Record responses
     to readings, raise questions, analyze major
     themes.

3.   Take responsibility for leading part of a
     discussion.

4.   Interview a Jewish woman (guidelines to be
     distributed).

5.   Participate in a Jewish event (cultural or re-
     ligious, traditional or transformed). Describe
     your experiences and analyze them in relation to
     the theoretical conceptions we have been dis-
     cussing all semester.

5.   Write a synthesis of your journal. This is to be
     a summary analysis of the development of your
     responses to the material over the course of the
     semester. What changes to you observe in your own
     thinking about the intersection of Judaism and
     feminism? Which new ideas most intrigued you and
     why?

SYLLABUS

Week 1.   Introductions, Expectations, Context Setting:

          The intersection of Judaism and Feminism,
          poem: "I am Woman," Malka Heifetz Tussman,
          Marcia Falk, trans. (hand-out) and Enid Dame,
          "Vilde Chaye," in Tribe of Dina, p. 170
          (hand-out).

Week 2.   The Laws that Bind: Jewish Law as the
          Foundation of Jewish Life

          "The Judaic Yoke," from Leslie Hazelton, The
          Israeli Woman: Myth and Reality.

          From On Being a Jewish Feminist:

               "The Jew Who Wasn't There: Halakha and
               the Jewish Woman," Rachel Adler, p. 12.

               "The Lilith Question," Aviva Cantor, p.
               40.

24

"Notes Towards Asking the Right Questions," Cynthia Ozick, p. 120.

"The Right Question is Theological," Judith Plaskow, p. 223.

"Language, God, and Liturgy," Judith Plaskow, Response 13:4 (Spring 1983), pp. 3-14.

Week 3.   Jewish Identity and Diversity: The Intersection of anti-Semitism, sexism, racism, homophobia, class bias, and other "differences" that disturb the apparent cohesion of "Jewish community": the Ashkenazi assumption, "Jew by birth" in tension with "Jew by choice," intermarriage and such themes.

"Between Invisibility and Overvisibility: The Politics of anti-Semitism in the Women's Movement and Beyond," Beck.

from Tribe of Dina:

"Nose is a Country," Aishe Berger, p. 126.

"Two Stories," Isabelle Maynard, p. 64.

"Choices: Frankfurt 1945," Irene Eber, p. 102.

"Short Black Hair," Jennifer Krebs, p. 98.

"Premonitions of Death," Adele Krebs, p. 100.

"To be a Hanu," Rita Arditti, p. 14.

Week 4.   Jewish Identity and Diversity (continued)

from Nice Jewish Girls: A Lesbian Anthology:

"Why is This Book Different from all other Books?" Evelyn Torton Beck, p. xiii.

all of section, "If I am not for myself, who will be?" pp. 5-46 (Greenfield, Kaye/Kantrowicz, Klepfisz).

all of section, "Jewish Identity: A Coat of Many Colors," pp. 55-98 (Segal, Bart, Wahba, Teubal, Rich, Mennis).

from Tribe:

"With Love, Lena," Teya Schaffer, p. 157.

"To Be an Arab Jew: Gevalt Poem," Nava Mizrahi, p. 211.

"An Interview with Chaya Shalom," p. 200.

Week 5.   Women and Language: Yiddish and Ladino

Women's prayers in Yiddish:

Tekhinot (Hand-out)

from Tribe:

essays and poems by Klepfisz: "Secular Jewish Identity: Yidishkayt in America," p. 30, "Di rayze aheym: the journey home," p. 49; "Etlekhe verter oyf mame-loshn: A few words in the mother tongue," p. 77; "Fradel Schtock," p. 152; Yiddish folk songs by Ruth Rubin, Martha Schlamme, Chava Alberstein.

Ladino: Judith Wachs, "The Heart of her People," in Tribe, p. 25.

Flora Jagody, "Kantikas di mi nona," Sung in Ladino. (Altarassa Records, 6307 Beachway Drive, Falls Church, VA 22044).

Susan Talve on the National Women's Studies Association Tape Jewish Feminist Voices (NWSA, LaSalle College, Philadelphia, PA).

26

Week 6. Women in the Shtetl

Deborah, Esther Kreitman (recently rediscovered text by the sister to the brothers Isaac Bashevis and I.J. Singer).

Week 7. Between Two Worlds

Bread Givers, Anzia Yezierska

Dakota Diaspora, Sophie Trupin

Francie Saposnik on NWSA tape

Week 8. Between Two Worlds

Tell Me a Riddle, Tillie Olsen

from A Leak in the Heart, Faye Moskowitz, Godine, 1985.

from Tribe:

"In This Country, But In Another Language, My Aunt Refuses to Marry the Men Everyone Wants Her To," p. 89.

Film: Yudie (New Day Films)

Week 9. Between Three Worlds: Europe, America and Israel

"Three Myths," Hazelton from Israeli Women in Heschel, p. 65.

Lea Majaro-Mintz, Sculptures; Gail Rubin Photographs.

"Next Year in Jerusalem," in Nice Jewish Girls, pp. 193-242.

"Interview with Lil Moed," in Tribe, pp. 256-263.

Film: Anu Banu: The Daughters of Utopia

Week 10.   The Holocaust and Women's Resistance

"Women Surviving the Holocaust," Katz and Ringlebaum.

Vera Laska, Women in the Resistance (Greenwood Press) (Hand-out)

Slides: Charlotte Salomon: Life or Theater?

Week 11.   Jews and Money

Gluckl of Hameln

Dona Gracia Di Nasi

Week 12.   Jews and Memory

Keeper of Accounts, Irena Klepfisz

Week 13.   Jews and Community: Feminist Possibilities

"Families and the Jewish Community," Response 14:4 (1985), pp. 5-20.

A Weave of Women, E.M. Broner.

Week 14.   Theory into Practice: Jewish Feminist Transformations

"Spirituality, Community, and Politics: B'Not Esh and the Feminist Reconstruction of Judaism," Martha Ackelsberg, Journal of Feminist Studies in Religion 2:2 (Fall 1986), pp. 109-120.

Week 15.   Summary and Synthesis. Sharing of Interviews and responses to Jewish Cultural or Religious Experiences.

CHILDREN OF SARAH: APPROACHES TO JEWISH WOMEN'S HISTORY AND SPIRITUALITY

Deborah Budner and Miriam Peskowitz
Oberlin College

This course was taught by Deborah Budner and Miriam Peskowitz as part of the Experimental College of Oberlin College, spring 1986. All of the participants in the class were undergraduates. The class met once a week for 90 minutes over a twelve-week period. In addition, class members gathered together once a week for a ritual.

Budner and Peskowitz were very gratified by the enthusiastic response of those who participated in this experimental course, and spent much of the following summer revising and restructuring the course to better meet the needs of future students of Jewish women's history and spirituality. What follows here is part of their introduction to this revised version of this encyclopedic course.

* * *

A Rough History of the Evolution of "Children of Sarah"

This course was conceived by two people who wanted to combine academic and personal exploration of Jewish women's issues. Both Miriam and I were Religion majors. Both of us had various experiences in Jewish women's spiritual groups - Rosh Hodesh rituals, conventions, etc., as well as in a gamut of conservative to innovative mixed gender spiritual groups. We felt the schism between the academic, critical, distanced approach and the spiritual, experiential route. But we also thought the two could and should be combined.

As we descended from the enthusiastic theoretical plans to pragmatic action we realized that we weren't sure how to combine spiritual and academic approaches and we weren't sure what we would find in looking at "history" and "spirituality" together. The name of the syllabus, "Children of Sarah: Approaches to Jewish Spirituality and Women's History," conveys our own hesitation about finding any clues of historical women's spirituality. We knew we could study Jewish spirituality and we knew we could study Jewish Women's History but we weren't sure where and if the two intersected. One of the most important things I have learned is how inextricably bound Jewish history and spirituality are. I think my Jewish education, as that of many American Jews of my generation, neglected to deal with spirituality—the experiencing of religion—not just the structures, laws, etc. This problem came out in our class discussions: How do we learn about the spirituality of others, of ourselves? How do we get to the root of spirituality? What is/was that first experience which was so powerful that it had to be preserved through community and law? Part of the feminist critique is that the preservation of this spirituality/religion has been too patriarchal. In trying to look beneath this we must give ourselves a certain authority. But then how does respect for the tradition fit in? If we only seek a women's "spiritual experience," what makes it Jewish instead of Christian, pagan, or Hindu feminist spirituality? Is Jewish women's spirituality Jewish because the women who are forming it are Jewish? Because there is something inherently Jewish about it? Because the forms of expression and ritual we use are historically Jewish?

It was our assumption that all these questions cannot be confronted without the knowledge of what has come before us. It was our hope that studying Jewish history would give us perspectives on previous genera- tions' modes of spirituality as well as give us his- torical precedents for our feminist project. And it would give us a sense of rootedness in the history and culture which included the experiences of women. Hopefully the links between history and spirituality become more apparent as one sees more of a relationship between herself and her history. Thus, the link between history and spirituality came along with the link between the academic and the personal.

We felt a responsibility to both feminist theory and process as well as to more traditional Jewish approaches. Feminist theory was translated into the emphasis on the diverse strands within Judaism (Hel- lenistic Judaism, Apocalyptic cults, Hasidism, verna- cular culture, etc.). We tried to stress that just as there is no monolithic "Jewish experience" there is no one monolithic "Jewish" approach. Jews have dealt with change and crisis in many different ways. Also, feminist theory asks questions about the way we study history. A more traditional approach has dwelled on the rabbis and the leaders of Jewish history.

30

The unnamed women and men fade away into the background. Recovering this faded history is crucial to fully understanding Jewish history.

Because we also wanted to be responsible to and respectful of Jewish tradition, we structured the class around the major phases of Jewish history. We were studying differing experiences of Jews from an insider's viewpoint --as people who felt some commitment to the history and culture, as people who had respect for it as well as critiques of it and quarrels with it. This issue of balancing acceptance and criticism became the most challenging for us as instructors and for the students.

The members of the class came from a variety of backgrounds. Some came to class much more interested in feminism than in Judaism. Many of these women had grown up with unaffirming or unmeaningful Jewish identities. They came to class, often, with little hesitance about questioning traditional assumptions, few inhibitions about "stepping on holy ground." This came out in discussions but especially in rituals. Because there was little knowledge or respect for what is commonly thought to be "Jewish," there was less threat when new ideas or rituals challenged the status quo. There were also people who came to the class with positive Jewish identities or who had embraced traditional Judaism on their own. They added to the class elements of faith and rootedness. But the two extremes, along with those who generally waded about in the middle, often conflicted. Challenging each other, threatening each other's assumptions, experimenting with different approaches to Rosh Hodesh, Passover, and Shabbat, was hard but fruitful and rewarding. It gave us all a clearer understanding of how challenging diversity can be within a community. In addition, these struggles served to reinforce what we had learned in our inquiry into Jewish history. Primary sources portrayed various responses to political, geographic, and cultural circumstances. Secondary sources, with their various biases and agendas, had given further clues about differing understandings of Jewish history/spirituality. I think that those who came into the course with little Jewish identification but much feminist identification came to see Judaism as more "theirs," as a tradition of which they are a part. Those who entered with a greater Jewish identity than feminist came to question their own assumptions about

31

Judaism. And all of us got a glimpse of how much there is for Jewish women to uncover, reject, reclaim and reshape.

* * *

Do these names mean anything to you: Huldah, Sambathe, B'ruriah, Gluckel of Hameln, Anzia Yezierska, Rebecca Tiktiner, Emma Goldman? Did you ever learn about Jewish folklore and astrology, Jewish mysticism and meditation? This course aims at recovering traditions and stories of Jewish culture and religion which have too often been ignored.

Through reading biographical and autobiographical accounts, we will seek to answer questions such as "Where were and who are the women in Jewish history?" and "What can we learn from the lives of both the exceptional "named" women and from the lives of those women whose names have been lost?"

Through discussion, we will examine the lives of our foremothers, attempting to uncover the lives and lifestyles of Jewish women past and present and using the experiences of our Jewish foremothers to shape our own experiences as Jewish women.

Through rituals and action, we will explore possibilities of integrating spirituality and women's experience into our observances of Shabbat, Rosh Hodesh (the Sanctification of the New Moon), and other traditional Jewish holidays.

The expectations for members of this course are: required readings, active participation in rituals and celebrations, one short discussion facilitation on a historical woman, and a creative project (art, dance, song, fiction, theatre, poetry, etc.) inspired by people, ideas, or issues discussed throughout the course.

Introduction

Some major issues, themes, and questions emerge while exploring Jewish women's spirituality and history.

1. Who has formed and molded Jewish religious traditions? Who has recorded Jewish history? From where is the authority to form, mold, and record traditions and history derived?

32

2. In looking at traditional sources, how do we uncover the assumptions and agendas of those who created these sources? What are the sources of information about women's history and spirituality? How do these sources, written and preserved by women, compare with those written and preserved by men?

3. Is there any "pure" Judaism? One theme of this course is to uncover the multitude of strands in Judaism, both the elite and popular religion and history, as well as to explore Judaism's interaction with other religious traditions.

4. How does traditional women's spirituality compare to traditional men's spirituality?

5. How have Jewish women historically balanced their identities as both Jews and women? Have these identities been integrated? Conflicted? How do we balance these aspects of our identity?

6. As Jewish feminists, can we find precedents in Jewish history for change and reinterpretation of Judaism?

7. How does tracing out Jewish women's history and spirituality affect our understanding of the traditional accounts of Jewish history? If we were to rewrite Jewish history, what would we emphasize? What approaches are more comprehensive and satisfactory? If we work to redefine Jewish spirituality, how will perspectives of women affect both the process and the conclusions? Does this process of reevaluating Jewish history give us new perspectives on what constituted "authority" in molding and recording Jewish religion and history?

Women in the Bible

For this session, each course participant should pick one woman from the Tanach and prepare a short presentation for class. Throughout the course, each individual will grapple with issues using her specific biblical woman; in effect, each of us will be in a personal relationship with a biblical woman during this course.

A General View of the Matriarchs

Reading:

> Genesis, focusing on the stories of women: Eve 2:18-3:24; Sarah 12:5-17, 16:1-18:15, 20:1-21:13, 23:1-3; Daughters of Lot 19:8-10; Hagar 16:1-16, 21:9-21, 25:12-18; Rebekah 24:1-14.67, 25:19-26, 27:5-17, 27:48-28.9; Keturah 25:1-4; Judith/ Basemath 26:34-35; Rachel 29:4-31, 30:1-26, 31:14-32; Bilhah 30:3-8; Zilpah 30:1-31; Dinah 34:1-31; Tamar 38:1-30.

> Phyllis Trible, ed., "Depatriarchalizing in Biblical Tradition," in Elizabeth Koltun, ed., The Jewish Woman: New Perspectives (N.Y.: Schocken, 1976), pp. 217-240.

> Phyllis Bird, "Images of Women in the Old Testament," in Rosemary Radford Ruether, Religion and Sexism (N.Y.: Simon and Schuster, 1974), pp. 41-88.

> Sondra Henry and Emily Taitz, Written Out of History (Fresh Meadows, NY: Biblio Press, 1983), Chapter 1: "The First Jewish Heroines--Biblical Women," pp. 15-29.

Recommended:

> Savina Teubal, Sarah the Priestess: The First Matriarch of Genesis (Ohio: Swallow Press, 1982).

Paradigms of Piety and Leadership

Reading:

> Miriam (Exodus 2, 15:20-21, Numbers 12, 20:1, Deuteronomy 24:8-9, Micah 6:4)

> Song of Deborah (Judges 4:5)

> Yael (Judges 4:17-24, 5:24-27)

> Song of Hannah (1 Samuel 1, 2)

> The Book of Ruth (in the Bible)

Phyllis Trible, Texts of Terror: Literary-Feminist Readings of Biblical Narratives (Philadelphia: Fortress Press, 1984).

T. Drorah Setel, "Prophets and Pornography: Female Sexual Imagery in Hosea," in Letty Russell, ed., Feminist Interpretation of the Bible (Philadelphia: Westminster Press, 1985).

Recommended:

Sheila Collins, A Different Heaven and Earth: A Feminist Perspective on Religion (Valley Forge, PA: Judson Press, 1974).

Early Judaism: 300 B.C.E.-100 C.E.

In the period of "early Judaism," Jews were faced with troublesome and challenging political, social, and religious situations--the development of the Temple cult in Jerusalem and the offering of sacrifices; the internal battles of different political sects--Pharisees, Sadducees, Revolutionaries, Scribes; the origins of the synagogue, reactions to the growing imperialism and political power of the Greek and later Roman Empires. Jews from varied backgrounds created different responses to these historical situations and political circumstances.

Responses to Life: Sectarian Judaism and Apocalyptic Cults

There was no monolithic Judaism. Instead, we see an abundance of communities, sects, and ideas: Essenes seeking religious purity, radical fringe groups, High Priests performing sacrifices, wilderness spiritual communities. This experience sets a precedent for a new, diversified and possibly feminist understanding of Jewish traditions and history - one in which a seemingly "normative" religion is not accepted.

This experience also shows us that it is only the existence of a "mainstream" which makes creative experimentation seem "marginal."

Reading:

> Enoch, concentrating on The Book of Watchers 1-36,
> in James Charlesworth, The Pseudepigrapha, Volume
> 1 (Garden City, NY: Doubleday, 1985).

> James Charlesworth, "Jewish Astrology in the
> Talmud, Pseudepigrapha, the Dead Sea Scrolls, and
> Early Palestinian Synagogues," in Harvard Theo-
> logical Review 70:3/4, July/Oct. 1977.

> Philo, The Contemplative Life in David Winston,
> tr., Philo of Alexandria (NY: Paulist Press,
> 1981).

> The Dead Sea Scrolls

Recommended:

> Erwin Goodenough, Jewish Symbols in the Greco-
> Roman World (Princeton: Princeton University
> Press, 1964), Volumes 9-12.

Jewish-Hellenistic Literature

Hellenistic Judaism covers the time period 300 B.C.E.
to 100 C.E., and the geographic area of the
Mediterranean Near East under the cultural, as well as
political, influence of the Greek and Roman Empires.
The term itself implies syncretism - the interplay
between cultural and religious systems whereby symbols,
imagery, concepts, and rituals are shared and borrowed.
The process of syncretism begs us to consider what the
essential parts of Judaism are--those that must be
maintained in order to stay "within" the confines of
the religion. Where do we draw the lines of borrowing
and syncretism? When have we strayed too far? How can
we apply the activity, texts, and literature of this
period to our own senses of Jewish spirituality and
religion?

Reading:

> Sybilline Oracles 3, 4, & 5 in James Charlesworth,
> Old Testament Pseudepigrapha - Volume 1 (Garden
> City, NY: Doubleday, 1985).

> Susannah, in the Apocrypha (sometimes this is
> called the story of Daniel and Susannah).

Judith, in the Apocrypha.

Esther, in the Bible.

"Joseph and Aseneth" in James Charlesworth, Old Testament Pseudepigrapha - Volume 2 (Garden City, NY: Doubleday, 1986).

Henry and Taitz, Written Out of History. Chapter 3: "Buried Treasures of Egypt and Greece," pp. 30-43.

Recommended:

Bernadette Brooten, Women Leaders in the Synagogue: Inscriptional Evidence and Background Issues (Georgia: Scholars Press, 1982).

Martin Hengel, Judaism and Hellenism (Philadelphia, Fortress Press, 1981).

Classical Judaism (200-1600)

This is the period in which the Rabbis emerge and the codification of the traditional and law takes place. What do we save, what can we reclaim? How do we approach this tradition of the learned elite--a tradition written by men?

The "Ideal Woman": How Jewish Law (Halakhah) Treats Women

Reading:

Rachel Biale, Women and Jewish Law: An Exploration of Women's Issues in Halakhic Sources (NY: Schocken, 1984), Introduction and Chapter 1: Women and the Mitzvot, pp. 3-44.

Judith Hauptman, "Images of Women in the Old Testament," in Ruether, Religion and Sexism (NY: Simon & Schuster, 1974).

Recommended:

Compare the feminist approach of Biale and Hauptmann with the non-feminist interpretations of Moses Meiselman, Jewish Women and Jewish Law (NY: Ktav, 1978, The Jewish Woman in Rabbinic

Literature: A Psychohistorical Perspective (NY: Ktav, 1985); and I. Epstein, "The Jewish Woman in the Responsa 900 C.E.--1500 C.E.," in Response: The Jewish Women's Anthology, Volume 18, Summer 1973, pp. 23-31.

Isaac Klein, ed., The Code of Maimonides: Book Four - The Book of Women (New Haven: Yale University Press, 1972).

Jewish Women's Realities

Examples from the Mediterranean World - Learned Women and Teachers

Reading:

Leonard Swidler, "Beruriah: Her World Became Law," Lilith, Spring/Summer 1977.

Henry and Taitz, Written out of History Chapter 4: "Daughters of the Talmud: Ima Shalom," pp. 44-5; Chapter 6: "Storehouse of Jewish Writings - the Cairo Geniza," pp. 71-82; Rebetzin Mizrachi, pp. 108-113; Scribes and Printers, pp. 114-122; Devorah Ascarelli, pp. 123-135; Sara Coppia Sullam, pp. 130-135.

Women's Public Lives: Politics and Economics

Reading:

Cecil Roth, The House of Nasi: Dona Gracia (Philadelphia: Jewish Publication Society, 1948).

Henry and Taitz, Written out of History Chapter 5: Poets and Warriors: Oases in the Desert--Kahinah, Kasmunah, Sarah. Chapter 10: Women of Influence-Benvenida Abrabanel, Dona Gracia Nasi, Anna the Hebrew, Esther Kura, Esperanza Malchi.

Women's Private Lives: Spirituality and Family Life

The Techines are prayers uttered and written in Yiddish, an Eastern European vernacular language, by and for women and less educated men. Those techines written for women often emphasized personal and familial concerns, or commemorated domestic observances of holidays and rituals. The Tzeenah U Rena is of similar origins. Known as "Women's Torah," it contains didactic retellings of Biblical stories. In these sources, what is the conception of the religious role of Jewish women? What kinds of spirituality are stressed for women, and how does this spirituality compare with that of men? From these sources, what can we tell about the Jewish woman's relationship with God? With other members of her community, both men and women?

Reading:

> Norman Gore, tr., Tzena U Rena (NY: Vantage Press, 1965).

> Techines - Jewish Women's Prayers, in Chava Weissler, "Voices from the Heart," in R. Siegel and C. Rheins, The Jewish Almanac (NY: Bantam Books, 1980), pp. 541-545.

> Henry and Taitz, Written Out of History, "The Anxious Letters," pp. 102-107, "The Prague Letters," pp. 152-164, "The Three Portals," pp. 184-200.

One Woman's Life

Autobiography as history--weaving a Jewish Woman's life together and meshing the ideal with the actual.

Reading:

> Marvin Lowenthal, tr., The Memoirs of Gluckel of Hameln (NY: Shocken, 1977) with special attention to pp. 1-10, 34-39, 84-89, 222-232, 271-277.

Responses to "Modernity"

Religious Movements

Hasidism: An Example From Eastern Europe 1700–1850

Hasidism was a social/religious revival movement which included the popularization of a mystical tradition which previously had been the domain of a learned elite. Hasidism also incorporated a great deal of Jewish "folk" religion: magic, amulets, chants, and folklore. In addition, hasidism brought changes in the structure of the Jewish community--deep splits occurred between those who were and weren't Hasidism, and Hasidic men would often geographically follow their "rebbes," leaving the women at home. Did Hasidim change the relation between Jewish classes and genders? How did it affect the issue of access to Jewish spirituality?

Reading:

Dan Ben-Amos and Jerome Mintz, eds., In Praise of the Baal Shem Tov (NY: Schocken, 1984). Look for the tales about women and witches.
Nachman of Breslov: The Tales (NY: Paulist Press, 1978).

"Lady Rabbis and Rabbinic Daughters," in H. Rabinowicz, The World of Hasidism, pp. 202-210.

"Ludomir, Maid of," in Encyclopedia Judaica.

Henry and Taitz, Written Out of History Chapter 7: One Step Ahead: Hasidic Women, pp. 175-183.

Secular Movements

Haskalah - An Example From Western Europe

Jewish Radical Circles - An Example From Eastern Europe

The assimilation of Jews into a secular community affected notions of Jewish community, identity, and religion. As well, the changes which secular modernity brought about affected men and women, and Jews of different economic classes, differently. How did women join in or reject these trends of assimilation? Did these secular movements change the roles of Jewish women? To what extent did Western European "Enlightenment" learning or Eastern European revolutionary activity provide for a change in roles, expectations, and lifestyles of Jewish women?

Reading:

"The Passion of Rahel Varnhagen," in Pamela White Hadas, In Light of Genesis (Philadelphia: Jewish Publication Society, 1980).

Marion Kaplan, "Bertha Pappenheim: Founder of German-Jewish Feminism," in Koltun, The Jewish Woman, pp. 149-163.

Hannah Arendt, Rahel Varnhagen: The Life of a Jewish Woman (NY: Harcourt Brace Jovanovich, 1974).

Nora Levin, While Messiah Tarried: Jewish Socialist Movements 1871-1917 (NY: Schocken, 1977).

Resistance to Destruction: The Holocaust

Reading:

Etty Hillesum, An Interrupted Life (NY: Simon & Schuster, 1984).

Vera Laska, ed., Women in the Resistance and in the Holocaust (Westport, CT: Greenwood Press, 1983).

Charlotte Salomon, Charlotte (NY: Viking Press, 1981).

The "New" Worlds

Jewish women left the villages, cities, and ghettoes of Europe and journeyed. Here are some of the stories of these women in the United States and Israel. For these women immigrants to the US, their experience varied by their specific class identification.

Jewish Women in 18th and 19th Century United States

An Example of Women in the German Reform Movement

A large part of the early American Jewish tradition was influenced by the German Reform movement. How were women treated by such communities which stressed "enlightenment"? How did these women self-identify in this liberal "Americanizing" movement? What role did they play in building the structures of this Jewish movement?

Reading:

Jacob Marcus, The American Jewish Woman: A Documentary History (NY: Ktav Publishing, 1981), Letters from Rebecca Samuel, pp. 42-46; from Rachel Mordechai, pp. 80-86; Poetry by Rebekhah Gumpert Hyneman, pp. 183-5; by Adah Isaacs Menken, pp. 273-85; by Penina Moise, pp. 124-128; by Emma Lazarus, pp. 325-328; Writings of Deborah Moses, p. 133; Judith Cohen's Code of Ethics, pp. 78-79; Ernestine Rose, pp. 162-169; Ray Frank, "Female Rabbi," pp. 380-383; Emil Hirsch, "The Modern Jewess," pp. 457-59' Myer Moses, pp. 64-66; Devotional Exercises for Women, pp. 178-182; A Plea for Religious Education for Women, pp. 225-228; Maud Nathan, "Sephardic Orthodoxy," pp. 268-272; Women in the Synagogue, pp. 282-298; Edna Ferber, pp. 373-379.

"Assimilation Was Their Goal: The German Jewish Woman in America" and "The Uptown Lady and the Downtown Woman: Two Kinds of Jews," in Charlotte Baum, Sonya Michel, and Paula Hyman, eds., The Jewish Woman in America (NY: New American Library, 1977), pp. 17-46, 163-186.

"The American Jewess 1895-1899," in History of Women's Periodicals (New Haven, CT: Research Publishers Inc.).

Recommended:

Ann Broude, "The Jewish Women's Encounter with American Culture," in Rosemary Radford Ruether and Rosemary Skinner Keller Women and Religion in America: The 19th Century (San Francisco: Harper & Row, 1981).

Eastern European Immigrants 1890-1939

Jewish Women as Workers and Radicals

Here we see Jewish women identifying not only as Jews and as women but also as workers and radicals. Investing great intensity and dedication into their tasks, they unionized the workplace and organized for radical political change. These Jewish women workers/radicals differed greatly from each other over religious orientation, culture, ideology, and communities. What were working class and radical intellectual Jewish women doing? How did being Jewish, being a woman, and being a worker or radical fit together or conflict?

Reading:

Emma Goldman, <u>Living My Life</u>.

Alice Kessler-Harris, "Organizing the Unorganizable: Three Jewish Women and their Union" in <u>Labor History</u> (Volume 17, Winter 1976, pp. 5-14).

June Sochen, "Radical Jewish Women Activists" in <u>Consecrate Every Day: The Public Lives of Jewish American Women 1890-1980</u> (Albany, NY: SUNY Press, 1981).

Sydney Weinberg, "Working Daughters," in <u>Lilith</u>: 8, pp. 20-23.

Sarah Schulman, "When We Were Very Young: A Walking Tour Through Radical Jewish Women's History on the Lower East Side 1879-1919" in <u>The Tribe of Dina</u> (Montpelier, VT: Sinister Wisdom Books, 1986), pp. 232-253.

"Weaving the Fabric of Unionism: Jewish Women Weave the Movement" in Baum, <u>et al.</u>, <u>The Jewish Woman in America</u>, pp. 121-162.

Gary Endelman, "Solidarity Forever: Rose Schneiderman and the Women's Trade Union League," Doctoral Dissertation, University of Delaware (Ann Arbor, MI: Xerox University Microfilm, June 1978).

R. Rosen and S. Davidson, <u>The Maimie Papers</u> (Westbury, NY: The Feminist Press, 1977). Focus on introduction, 191-215, 158-172, 99-133.

Jacob Marcus, The American Jewish Woman: A Documentary History (NY: Ktav, 1981); "Bintel Briefs--Letters to the Editor of the Daily Forward," pp. 529-537; Clara Lemlich - Union Leader, p. 568-580; The Triangle Shirt Waist Fire, pp. 590-595; Margaret Sanger, pp. 677-681; Polly Adler, pp. 690-697.

Background Reading:

Irving Howe, World of Our Fathers (NY: Simon & Schuster, 1976).

Moses Rischin, The Promised City: New York's Jews 1870-1914 (Cambridge, Harvard University Press, 1962).

Jewish Women as Writers

This was the first generation of Jewish women to take themselves seriously as writers. Yet, as writers, these women were also misunderstood and neglected. How did they struggle with their place as women within a changing Judaism and within a changing world? How does their literature portray this? Much of their literature deals with themes of alienation as Jews in America--what do their perspectives add to our understanding of the immigrant experience?

Reading:

Anzia Yezierska, "The Lord Giveth," from The Open Cage: an Anzia Yezierska Collection, Alice Kessler-Harris, ed. (NY: Persea Books, 1979).

Anzia Yezierska, Bread Givers: A Struggle Between a Father of the Old World and a Daughter of the New World (NY: Persea Books, 1975).

Anzia Yezierska, Hungry Hearts and Other Stories (NY: Persea Books, 1975).

Mary Antin, The Promised Land: the Autobiography of a Russian Immigrant (Princeton University Press, 1985).

Adrienne Cooper, "About Anna Margolin," in The Tribe of Dina, pp. 146-151.

Howard Schwartz and Anthony Rudolf, eds., Voices in the Ark: The Modern Jewish Poets (NY: Avon Press, 1980) Rayzel Zychlinska, p. 375; Miriam Vlinover, p. 366; Malka Heifetz Tussman, pp. 360-362; Rachel Boimwell, p. 248; Anna Margolin, pp. 312-314; Aysa, pp. 244-246.

Norma Fain Pratt, "Anna Margolin's Lider: A Study in Women's History, Autobiography and Poetry," in Walden, Jewish Women Writers and Jewish Women in Jewish Literature (Albany, NY: SUNY Press).

Norma Fain Pratt, "Culture and Radical Politics: Yiddish Women Writers 1980-1940," in American Jewish History, 70/1 (Sept. 1980), pp. 68-90.

Jewish Women as Immigrants to Israel

What was/is the role of women in a national liberation movement? How were the concerns of women incorporated into the cultural and political creation of Israel?

Reading:

Rachel Katznelson, The Plough Woman: Memoirs of Pioneer Women of Palestine (NY: Herzl Press, 1975).

Dafna N. Izraeli, "The Zionist Women's Movement in Palestine 1911-1927: A Sociological Analysis," in Signs, Autumn 1981.

Else Lasker Schuler, Hebrew Ballads and Other Poems (Philadelphia, Jewish Publication Society, 1980).

Myra Glazer, ed., Burning Air and a Clear Mind: Israeli Women's Poetry (Athens, OH: Ohio University Press, 1983) Leah Goldberg, p. 4; Shirley Kaufman, p. 98; Rivka Miriam, p. 86; Dahlia Ravikovich, p. 34; Chaya Shenhav, p. 30; Shlomit Cohen, pp. 22-27.

Modern Jewish Feminism

Connecting and transforming knowledge, history, and traditions into personal practice and understandings.

Our Grandmothers and Mothers

We are directly connected to certain Jewish women. What are their stories? What do we give to them? What have they given us?

Reading:

Kim Chernin, In My Mother's House (NY: Harper & Row, 1983).

Jayne Sorkin, "Ima," and Irena Klepfisz, tr., "Fradel Schtok," in The Tribe of Dina, pp. 121-123 and 176-179.

Barbara Meyerhoff, "Bubbes and Zeydes: Old and New Roles for Elderly Jews," in J. Hoch-Smith, Women in Ritual and Symbolic Roles (NY: Simon & Schuster, 1978).

Sydelle Kramer and Jenny Mazur, Jewish Grandmothers (Boston: Beacon Press, 1976).

The Tribe of Dina, p. 146, p. 148, p. 176.

Jewish Feminist Theology and God Language

How do we create new feminist theologies? Can there be Jewish "theology"? What does experimentation with feminist God language involve? How do we interpret sacred texts using a feminist methodology?

Reading:

Marcia Falk, "What About God?," in Moment 33, March 1985.

Judith Plaskow, "Language, God and Liturgy: A Feminist Perspective," in Response 13/4, Spring 1983.

Judith Plaskow, "The Right Question is Theological," in Susannah Heschel, ed., On Being a Jewish Feminist (NY: Schocken, 1983).

Cynthia Ozick, "Notes Toward Finding the Right Question," in Heschel, On Being a Jewish Feminist (NY: Schocken, 1983).

Israeli Feminism

What is the Israeli feminist critique of Israel? What do various elements of Israeli society—religious, Sfardi, Ashkenazi, secular—have to say about the places of women and feminism in their society?

Reading:

P'nina Lahav, "Raising the Status of Women Through Law: The case of Israel," in Signs Fall 1977, pp. 193-209.

Lesley Hazelton, Israeli Women: The Reality Behind the Myth (NY: Simon & Schuster, 1977).

Shulamit Aloni, "Israel: Up the Down Escalator," in Robin Morgan, Sisterhood is Global (Garden City, NY: Anchor Books, 1984).

Natalie Rein, Daughters of Rachel: Women in Israel (NY: Penguin Books, 1979).

Geraldine Stern, Israeli Women Speak Out (Philadelphia: Lippincott, 1979).

Weaving Together Spirit and Theory

Creating New Stories—the Process of Midrash

Midrash is a traditional process whereby new stories are created to infuse new life, meaning, and ideas into older stories. In this manner, the collection of Jewish folklore continues to grow. As women, we have continued this Jewish tradition of midrash, incorporating our experiences into the tales and stories which we have inherited. Yet, how does our continued re-evaluation of Jewish lore, stories, and ideals challenge traditional understandings of Midrash?

Reading:

Barry Holtz, "Midrash," in Holtz, ed., Back to the Sources (NY: Summit Books, 1984), pp. 177-212.

"Midrash," Encyclopedia Judaica.

Compare (1) Marcia Falk, Love Letters From the Bible (NY: Harcourt, Brace, Jovanovich); (2) Song of Songs (in the Bible).

Compare (1) Aviva Cantor, "The Lilith Question," in Lilith Magazine Fall 1976; "Lilith," in Gershom Scholem, The Kabbalah; (3) Judith Plaskow, "Epilogue: The Coming of Lilith," in Ruether, Religion and Sexism, pp. 341-344; (4) Barbara Black Koltuv, The Book of Lilith (York Beach, ME: Nicholas-Hays, 1986).

Miriam's Timbrel, "A Woman's Hagadah," (Oberlin, OH: Oberlin College Women & Judaism/Hillel, 44074, 1984).

Compare (1) Judith Stein, "On Lesbian Invisibility: A Midrash for Shavuos," (Cambridge, MA: Boobeh Meiseh Press, 1984); (2) The Book of Ruth (in the Bible).

Compare (1) Penina Adelman, "Tamar: The Tree of Life," in Reconstructionist Magazine, Jan./Feb. 1986; (2) Genesis 38:1-30 (Tamar in the Bible).

Merle Field, "In A Different Voice," in Journal of Feminist Studies of Religion, 1/2 (Fall 1985), pp. 89-90 and Chava Weissler, "Standing at Sinai," in Journal of Feminist Studies of Religion, 1/2 (Fall 1985), pp. 91-92.

Enid Dame, "Lot's Wife Revisited," in The Tribe of Dina, pp. 168-169.

Ellen Gruber Garvey, "How is this Week Different? New York City Transit Strike: Spring 1980," in The Tribe of Dina, p. 172.

Pamela White Hadas, In Light of Genesis.

Compare (1) Mary Gendler, "The Restoration of Vashti," in Koltun, The Jewish Woman, pp. 241-247 and (2) The Book of Esther.

Creating New Rituals

Ritual can be the periodic and cyclical recreation of formative spiritual events and moments, as well as the creation of new spiritual space and time. How have modern Jewish women created lively and meaningful new rituals and observances? How have we applied our experiences as women and feminists into traditional Jewish holidays and life cycle commemorations?

Reading:

Penina Adelman, Miriam's Well: Rituals for Jewish Women Around the Year (NY: Biblio Press, 1986).

E.M. Broner, "Honor and Ceremony in Women's Rituals," in Charlene Spretnak, ed., The Politics of Women's Spirituality (NY: Anchor Press, 1982).

Arlene Agus, "This Month is For You: Observing Rosh Hodesh as a Women's Holiday," in Koltun, The Jewish Woman.

Phyllis Berman, "Enter A Woman," in Menorah: Sparks of Jewish Renewal 7/1-2 (Nov./Dec. 1985); and Judith Plaskow, "Bringing a Daughter into the Covenant," in Carol Christ and Judith Plaskow, eds., Womanspirit Rising.

Naomi Janowitz and Maggie Wenig, "Sabbath Prayers for Women," in Christ and Plaskow, eds., Womanspirit Rising.

Aviva Cantor, "A Jewish Woman's Haggadah," in Christ and Plaskow, eds., Womanspirit Rising.

A Multitude of Jewish Women's Lifestyles

Opening up to and respecting various Jewish women's cultures, nationalities, lifestyles and levels of religious observance.

Reading:

Blu Greenberg, On Women and Judaism: A View From Tradition (Philadelphia: Jewish Publication Society, 1981).

Lis Harris, "Sheina," in Holy Days: The World of a Hasidic Family (NY: Summit Books, 1985).

49

Adrienne Rich, "Split at the Root," and Susan Wolfe, "Jewish Lesbian Mothers," in Evelyn Torton Beck, Nice Jewish Girls: A Lesbian Anthology (Trumansburg, NY: Crossing Press, 1982), pp. 67-84 and 164-173.

Irena Klepfisz, "Secular Jewish Identity: Yidish-kayt in America," in The Tribe of Dina, pp. 30-48.

Chutzpah: A Jewish Liberation Anthology (San Francisco: New Glide Publications, 1977).

E.M. Broner, A Weave of Women (NY: Bantam Books, 1978).

Rita Arditti, "To Be A Hanu," and Judith Wachs, "The Heart of Her People," in The Tribe of Dina, pp. 14-29.

Alice Bloch, The Law of Return (Boston: Alyson Publications, 1983).

Rachel Biale, "Niddah--Laws of the Menstruant," and "Sexuality Outside of Marriage: Incest, Adultery, Promiscuity, and Lesbianism," in Women and Jewish Law (NY: Schocken, 1984), pp. 197-174 and 175-197.

Jewish Feminist Identity and Community--All That We Are

What is a "Jewish Feminist Community"? What are the expectations? What are the possibilities? What is the place of rituals in Jewish women's communities? How do we balance tradition and innovation? What kind of leadership is appropriate for our communities and rituals? Do we have visions of community and spirituality for the future?

What is the place of separatism in our communities? What is our relation to/with men? To/with other communities? Do we stay as a marginal sect or do we connect with other Jews?

What implications does feminism have for Judaism? What implications does Judaism have for feminism? What is our position within the women's community? Within the feminist spirituality community?

Reading:

Letty Cottin Pogrebin, "Anti-Semitism in the Women's Movement," Ms. Magazine, June 1982.

Elly Bulkin, Minnie Bruce Pratt, and Barbara Smith, Yours in Struggle: Three Feminist Perspectives on Anti-Semitism and Racism (Ithaca, NY: Firebrand Press, 1984).

Melanie Kaye/Kantrowitz, "To Be a Radical Jew in the Late Twentieth Century," in The Tribe of Dina pp. 264-287.

Beverly Smith, Judith Stein, Priscilla Golding, "The Possibility of Life Between Us: A Dialogue Between Black and Jewish Women," Conditions: 7, 1981.

Judith Plaskow, "Blaming Jews for the Birth of Patriarchy," and Annette Daum, "Death of the Goddess," from Nice Jewish Girls: A Lesbian Anthology, Evelyn Torton Beck, ed., pp. 250-254 and 255-261.

51

WOMEN IN JEWISH CIVILIZATION

Sue Levi Elwell
University of Cincinnati

This one-semester course was cross-listed by the departments of Judaic Studies and Women's Studies. It met for three fifty-minute sessions each week.

* * *

Course description:

This course examines images of women in Jewish literature, law and liturgy from rabbinic times to the present and contrasts those images with the realities of Jewish women's lives as reflected in their writings and in contemporary social and historical accounts. During the quarter students will analyze the roles and activities of Jewish women as a discrete group within Jewish populations throughout the ages and consider the achievements and influence of several notable Jewish women.

Course requirements:

This course is conducted as a lecture-seminar, and students should be prepared to participate actively in discussions. Grades are based on class participation and on two written projects. The first project, 3-5 pages long, is a written response to a question on some aspect of women in/and Jewish law. The final project involves an in-class presentation and a written research report prepared in consultation with the instructor.

Tests:

Course readings are divided into two categories: basic (required) readings and additional (recommended) readings. All basic readings are drawn from the REQUIRED texts:

Baum, Hyman and Michel, The Jewish Woman in America
    (NY: Plume, 1976).
Elizabeth Koltun, ed., The Jewish Woman: New Perspectives (Philadelphia: Jewish Publication Society, 1976).

In addition to the required texts, the following books
are recommended:

Jacob Neusner, The Way of Torah: An Introduction to
    Judaism (third edition) (Belmont, CA: Duxbury).
    Particularly recommended for those who are new to
    the discipline of Judaic Studies.
Sondra Henry and Emily Taitz, Written Out of History
    (Fresh Meadows, NY: Biblio, 1984).
Aviva Cantor, The Jewish Woman Bibliography (NY:
    Biblio, 1980).
Blu Greenberg, On Women and Judaism (Philadelphia:
    Jewish Publication Society, 1981). A tradition-
    alist's view.
Julia Mazow, ed., The Woman Who Lost Her Names (NY:
    Harper & Row, 1980). Jewish women's writings.

                SYLLABUS (by weeks, more or less)

I.   Jewish Women in Jewish Law.

        Basic Readings:

        Selections from the Mishnah.
        Judith Hauptman, "Images of Women in the
            Talmud," Religion and Sexism, Rosemary R.
            Ruether, ed. (NY: Simon and Schuster,
            1974), pp. 184-212.
        Saul Berman, "The Status of Women in Halakhic
            Judaism," in Koltun.
        Anne Goldfeld, "Women as Sources of Torah in the
            Rabbinic Tradition," in Koltun.

        Additional Readings:

        Neusner, Chapters 14 and 15.
        Blu Greenberg, On Women and Judaism
            (Philadelphia: Jewish Publication Society,
            1981).
        Leonard Swidler, Women in Judaism: The Status
            of Women in Formative Judaism (Philadel-
            phia: Scarecrow Press, 1978).
        David Feldman, Marital Relations, Birth Control
            and Abortion in Jewish Law (NY: Schocken
            Books, 1974).

II.   Jewish Women in the Premodern World

Basic Readings:

Jacob R. Marcus, The Jew in the Medieval World
       NY: Atheneum, 1974), Sections 60, 79, 90
       and 94.
Gluckel, The Memoirs of Gluckel of Hameln,
       Marvin Lowenthal, trans. (NY: Schocken
       Books, 1977), pp. 1-5; 23-38; 95-99;
       222-230.

Additional Readings:

Henry and Taitz, Chapters 5-10.
Shlomo Goitein, A Mediterranean Society: The
       Jewish Communities of the Arab World as
       Portrayed in the Documents of the Cairo
       Geniza, Vol. III: The Family (Berkeley:
       University of California, 1978), pp.
       160-359.
Neusner, Chapter 18.
Cecil Roth, Dona Gracia and the House of Nasi
       (Philadelphia: Jewish Publication Society,
       1977).
Baum, Hyman and Michel, Chapter 1.

III.   Ghetto and Emancipation: The Western European
       Experience

Basic Readings:

Michael Meyer, The Origins of the Modern Jew
       (Detroit: Wayne State University Press,
       1967), pp. 85-114.
Marion Kaplan, "Women's Strategies in the Jewish
       Community in Germany," New German Critique
       14 (Spring 1978), 109-118.
Marion Kaplan, "Bertha Pappenheim: Founder of
       German-Jewish Feminism," in Koltun.

Additional Readings:

Marion Kaplan, The Jewish Feminist Movement in
       Germany: The Campaigns of the Judischer
       Frauenbund, 1904-1938 (Westport, CN:
       Greenwood Press, 1979).
Hannah Arendt, Rahel Varnhagen: The Life of a
       Jewish Woman (New York: Harcourt Brace
       Jovanovich, 1974).

Henry and Taitz, pp. 195-206.
Jacob Katz, "Family Kinship, and Marriage Among
Ashkenazim in the Sixteenth to Eighteenth
Centuries," Jewish Journal of Sociology I
(1959), 4-22.

IV.   Ghetto and Emancipation: The Eastern European
Experience

Basic Readings:

The following selections from Lucy Davidowicz,
ed., The Golden Tradition: Jewish Life and
Thought in Eastern Europe (Boston: Beacon
Press, 1967):
Pauline Wengeroff, "Memoirs of a
Grandmother," pp. 160-168.
Sarah Schenirer, "Mother of the Beth
Jacob Schools," pp. 206-209.
Puah Rakowski, "A Mind of My Own," pp.
388-393.
Deborah Weissman, "Bais Yaakov: A Historical
Model for Jewish Feminists," in Koltun.
"Voices From the Heart: Women's Devotional
Prayers," Chava Weissler, The Jewish
Almanac (NY: Bantam, 1980).
Baum, Hyman and Michel, Chapter 3.

Additional Readings:

Henry and Taitz, Chapter 13.

V.   Jewish Women in America: The Uptown Ladies

Basic Readings:

Baum, Hyman and Michel, Chapter 2.
Susan Dworkin, "Henrietta Szold: Liberated
Woman," in Koltun.
Hannah G. Solomon, A Sheaf of Leaves (Chicago:
Privately Printed, 1911), pp. 103-127.

Additional Readings:

Joan Dash, Summoned to Jerusalem: The Life of
Henrietta Szold (New York: Harper and Row,
1979).
Rudolf Glanz, The Jewish Woman in America: Two
Female Immigrant Generations (Vol. II: The
German Jewish Woman) (NY: Ktav, 1977).

Anita Libman Lebeson, Recall to Life: The
    Jewish Woman in America (South Brunswick,
    NJ: Thomas Yoseloff, 1970).
Rebekah Kohut, My Portion (NY: Albert and
    Charles Boni, 1925) or More Yesterdays (NY:
    Bloch Publishing Co., 1974).
Hannah Solomon, Fabric of My Life (NY: Bloch
    Publishing Co., 1974).

VI.   Jewish Women in America: The Downtown Women

Basic Readings:

Baum, Hyman and Michel, Chapters 4 and 5.
Anzia Yezierska, "The Lord Giveth," The Open
    Cage: An Anzia Yezierska Collection, Alice
    Kessler-Harris, ed. (NY: Persea, 1979).

Additional Readings:

Hutchins Hapgood, "The Old and New Woman," in
    The Spirit of the Ghetto (NY: Funk and
    Wagnalls, 1902).
Sydelle Kramer and Jenny Masur, eds., Jewish
    Grandmothers (Boston: Beacon Press, 1976).
Rudolph Glanz, The Jewish Woman in America (Vol.
    I: The Eastern European Jewish Woman) (NY:
    Ktav, 1976).
Any of the novels of Mary Antin and/or Anzia
    Yezierska.
Elizabeth Stern, I Am A Woman and A Jew (NY:
    J.H. Sears, 1926).

VII.   Jewish Women in America: The Second and Third
       Generation: 1950-1970

Basic Readings:

Baum, Hyman and Michel, Chapters 6 and 7.
Zena Smith Blau, "In Defense of the Jewish
    Mother," The Ghetto and Beyond, Peter I.
    Rose, ed. (NY: Random House, 1969), pp.
    57-68.
Pauline Bart, "Portnoy's Mother's Complaint," in
    Koltun.
Articles and excerpts on volunteerism from
    Lilith: 5 (1978), pp. 16-22.

VIII. Placing Women in Modern Jewish History: the Holocaust

Each student will read all or selections from one of the following:

Helena Birenbaum, Hope is the Last to Die (NY: Twayne Publishers, 1977).
Charlotte Delbo, None of Us Will Return (Boston: Beacon Press, 1978).
Fania Fenelon, Playing for Time (NY: Berkeley Publishing Co., 1977).
Livia Jackson, Elli: Coming of Age in the Holocaust (NY: New York Times Books, 1980).
Gerda Klein, All But My Life (NY: Hill and Wang, 1957).
Ella Lingens-Reiner, Prisoners of Fear (London: Gollancz, 1948).
Vladka Meed, On Both Sides of the Wall: Memoirs of the Warsaw Ghetto (Tel Aviv: Lohamei ha Ghettaot, 1972).
Judith Sternberg-Newman, In the Hell of Auschwitz (NY: Exposition Press, 1963).

Placing Women in Modern Jewish History: Israel

Basic Readings:

Shulamit Aloni, "The Status of the Women in Israel," Judaism 22:2 (Spring 1973), 248-256).
Marcia Freedman, "Israel: What's a Radical Feminist doing in a Place Like This?" Psychology of Women Quarterly 2:4 (Spring 1978), 355-362.
Roundtable Discussion on Women in Jewish Law, Israel Today, 24 August 1979, 10-14.
Carol Clapsaddle, "Flight from Feminism: The Case of the Israeli Women," in Koltun.
Rachel Janait, "Stages," in Koltun.

Additional Readings:

Rachel K. Shazar, The Plough Woman: Memoirs of the Pioneer Women of Palestine (NY: Herzl Press, 1975).
Lesley Hazelton, Israeli Women: The Reality Behind the Myths (NY: Simon and Schuster, 1977).
Neusner, Chapter 9.

IX.   Issues of the 1970's: Women in Jewish Life

Basic Readings:

Blu Greenberg, "Judaism and Feminism," in
    Koltun.
Steven M. Cohen, et al., "The Changing (?) Role
    of Women in Jewish Communal Affairs," in
    Koltun.
Laura Geller and Elizabeth Koltun, "Single and
    Jewish," in Koltun.
Cherie Koller-Fox, "Women and Jewish Education:
    A New Look at Bat Mitzvah," in Koltun.
Evelyn Torton Beck, "Why is this Book different
    from all other Books?" from Nice Jewish
    Girls: A Lesbian Anthology (Watertown, MA:
    Persephone Press, 1982).

Additional Readings:

Anne Lapidus Lerner, "Who Hast Not Made Me a
    Man: The Movement for Equal Rights for
    Women in American Jewry," American Jewish
    Yearbook 77 (1977), 3-28).
Amy Stone, "The Jewish Establishment is not an
    equal opportunity Employer," Lilith 1:4
    (Fall/Winter 77/78), 25-26.
Shirley Frank, "The Population Panic: Why
    Jewish Leaders want Jewish Women to be
    Fruitful and Multiply," Lilith 1:4
    (Fall/Winter 77/78), 12-17.

X.   Issues of the 1980's: Women in Jewish Ritual

Basic Readings:

Esther Ticktin, "A Modest Beginning," in Koltun.
Rachel Adler, "Tumah and Taharah: Ends and
    Beginnings," in Koltun.
Myra and Daniel Leifer, "On the Birth of a
    Daughter," in Koltun.
Arlene Agus, "This Month is for You," in Koltun.
Aviva Cantor Zuckoff, Jewish Women's Haggadah,"
    in Koltun.
Daniel Leifer, "On Writing New Ketubot,"
    in Koltun.
Judith Plaskow, "God and Feminism," Menorah 3:2
    (Feb. 1982), and responses in Menorah 3:3.
"How to get where we want by the year 2000,"
    Lilith: 7 (1980).

Additional Readings:

Susannah Heschel, "No Doors, No Guards: From
    Jewish Feminism to A New Judaism," Menorah
    4:1-2 (March 1983).
Nessa Rapoport, Preparing for Sabbath (NY: Wm.
    Morrow, 1981).

JEWISH WOMEN'S HISTORY

Edward R. Zweiback Levenson
Gratz College

This short course was designed for an intensive five-week summer session. Classes met twice a week for meetings lasting 2 1/2 hours. Class participants included both undergraduates and adults who took the course on a non-credit basis.

An earlier version of this syllabus appeared in the first edition of the Guide.

* * *

Course description:

The course will be devoted to a study of the image, roles, status, and activities of the Jewish woman in society in successive ages, as well as of the influence and contributions of individual female leaders. Attention will be paid to the Jewish and non-Jewish historical and cultural contexts. After studying the historical realities, we shall analyze current problems relating to the implementation of change in Jewish religion and life.

The grade will be determined on the basis of a take-home final examination due on July 26 and informed class discussion. Class texts are:

> Blu Greenberg, On Women and Judaism: A View from Tradition. (Philadelphia: Jewish Publication Society, 1981).

> Elizabeth Koltun, ed., The Jewish Woman: New Perspectives (NY: Schocken, 1976).

> Anzia Yezierska, The Open Cage: An Anzia Yezierska Collection (NY: Persea, 1979).

Week 1.   Introduction. God as Female. Our Mother in Heaven. The Ancient Near East. The Biblical and Intertestamental Periods.

Readings:

R. Harris and P. Trible, "Women in the Ancient
    Near East; Women in the Old Testament,"
    Interpreters' Dictionary of the Bible Supple-
    ment, 960-965.

Mary Gendler, "The Restoration of Vashti," The
    Jewish Woman, 241-247.

Phyllis Trible, "Depatriarchalizing in Biblical
    Interpretation," The Jewish Woman, 217-240.

Blu Greenberg, On Women and Judaism, 3-37,
    157-178.

Week 2.   The Talmudic Period. Women in Jewish Law:
    the Development of the Traditional Rabbinic
    Stances about Women and Marriage, Divorce,
    Religious Observance, Ritual Purity, Witness-
    ing, and Civil Status.

Readings:

Selections from the Mishnah and Gemara, and
    Maimonides' Book of Women.

Blu Greenberg, On Women and Judaism, 39-155.

Anne Goldfeld, "Women as Sources of Torah in the
    Rabbinic Tradition," The Jewish Woman,
    257-271.

Paula Hyman, "The Other Half;"
Saul Berman, "The Status of Women in
    Halakhic Judaism;" and
Esther Ticktin, "A Modest Beginning,"
    all in The Jewish Woman, 105-135.

Week 3.   Women in Medieval Times: Islamic and Chris-
    tian Worlds; Noteworthy Women and Challenges
    Faced. The Modern Age: Western Europe and
    Eastern Europe.

Readings:

Jacob R. Marcus, The Jew in the Medieval World,
    Sections 28, 35, 60, 79, 81, 90, 94.

Michael A. Meyer, "Rationalism and Romanticism:
Two Roads to Conversion," The Origins of the
Modern Jew, (Dorothea Schlegel, Henrietta
Herz, Rachel von Varnhagen), pp. 85-114.

Marion Kaplan, "Bertha Pappenheim: Founder of
German-Jewish Feminism," and Deborah
Weissman, "Bais Yaakov," The Jewish Woman,
pp. 139-163.

Week 4.   The American Experience: First and Second
Generations. Organization Women. The
"Jewish Mother." The Holocaust and
Resistance.

Readings:

Anzia Yezierska, The Open Cage.

Yuri Suhl, They Fought Back (Nuita Teitelboim,
Zofia Yamaika, Mala Zimetbaum, Rosa Robota),
pp. 51-54, 77-81, 182-188, 219-226.

Week 5.   Women in Eretz Yisrael. Current Issues.

Readings:

Selections from The Plough Women: Memoirs of the
Pioneer Women of Palestine, Rachel Katznelson
Shazar, ed.

Rachel Janait, "Stages," and Carol Clapsaddle,
"Flight from Feminism: The Case of the
Israeli Women," The Jewish Woman, pp.
171-175, 202-213.

"Female Baby Naming Ceremonies," "Women and Jewish
Education," "Rosh Hodesh Observances,"
"Jewish Women's Haggadah," The Jewish Woman,
pp. 19-71, 84-102.

Reena S. Friedman, "The Politics of Ordination,"
Lilith 6, pp. 9-15.

# # #

Take-home final examination

Kindly write brief essays, indicating a grasp of the most important respective contributions and critiques, on three of the following topics.

1. Blu Greenberg's synthesis of traditional Judaism and feminism.

2. Anzia Yezierska's description of Jewish immigrant women's experience.

3. The Jewish Woman--any "new perspectives" you wish to describe, on the basis of the Koltun book, et al., in history and today.

4. a. Lesley Hazelton's appraisal of the position of women in Israeli society in her Israeli Women: the Reality Behind the Myths (NY: Simon and Schuster, 1977).

(You may choose one or two among a, b, and c, if you select #4)   b. The uniqueness of Jewish women's experience, using selections from Julia Wolf Mazow's The Woman Who Lost Her Names: Selected Writings by American Jewish Women (San Francisco: Harper and Row, 1980).

c. Moshe Meiselman's defense of traditionalistic Judaism against feminism criticism, in his Jewish Woman in Jewish Law (NY: Ktav, 1978).

63

EVOLVING ROLES OF JEWISH WOMEN

Rela Geffen Monson
Gratz College
Bryn Mawr College

This is an updated version of Monson's course in the first edition of the Guide, and has been taught at both Gratz College and nearby Bryn Mawr.

* * *

I. Course Description - The objective of this course is to use the tools of sociological analysis to understand the evolution of women's roles in Judaism throughout history with particular emphasis on the contemporary American Jewish Community.

II. Books required for purchase: Elizabeth Koltun, ed., The Jewish Woman (Schocken Books, 1978) (TJW in assignments), Susannah Heschel, ed., On Being A Jewish Feminist (Schocken Books, 1983) (OBJF in assignments) and Susan Weidman Schneider, Jewish and Female (Simon and Schuster, 1985) (JF in assignments).

III. Requirements - There will be a midterm examination during session 7 (March 6). Students will also be required to complete a 10-15 page research paper related to the course on a topic approved by the instructor after the midterm.

IV. Weekly Topics and Assignments

January 23 - Introduction
            Plaskow: "The Jewish Feminist: Con-
            flict in Identities" (TJW:
              3-10)
            Cantor: "The Lilith Question" (OBJF:
            40-50)
            Schneider: "Introduction" (JF: 19-32)

January 30 - Jewish Women in the Biblical Period
            Trible: "Depatriarchalizing in Biblical
            Interpretation" (TJW: 217-240)
            Gendler: "The Restoration of Vashti"
            (TJW: 241-247)
            Kuzmack: "Aggadic Approaches to
            Biblical Women" (TJW: 248-256)

64

February 6 - Women in Halachic Judaism I
            Hymen: "The Other Half" (TJW: 105-114)
            Adler: "The Jew Who Wasn't There"
            (OBJF: 12-18)
            Schneider: "Law and Leadership" (JF:
            60-83)

February 13 - Women in Halachic Judaism II
            Adler: "Tumah and Taharah" (TJW:
            63-71)
            Berman: "The Status of Women in
            Halachic Judaism" (TJW: 114-128)
            Schneider: "From Observer to
            Participant" (JF: 60-83)

February 20 - The Jewish Feminist Movement of the '70's
            Ozick: "Notes Towards Finding the
            Right Question" (OBJF: 120-151)
            Greenberg: "Judaism and Feminism"
            (TJW: 179-92)

February 27 - Feminist Theology and Review
            Plaskow: "The Right Question is
            Theological" (OBJF: 223-234)
            Christ: "Women's Liberation and the
            Liberation of God" (TJW: 11-21)
            Gross: "Steps Toward Feminine Imagery
            of Deity in Jewish Theology"
            (OBJF: 234-247)
            Green: "Brides, Spouse, Daughter"
            (OBJF: 248-260)

March 6 -   Midterm Examination in Class

March 20 -   Women in Israeli Society
            Clapsaddle: "Flight From Feminism"
            (TJW: 202-217)
            Hazelton: "Israeli Women: Three
            Myths" (OBJF: 65-87)
            Janait: "Stages" (TJW: 171-178)

March 27 -   Changing Roles in American Religious
            Movements
            Reguer: "Kaddish" (OBJF: 171-177)
            Lipstadt: "And Deborah Made Ten"
            (OBJF: 207-209)
            Geller: "Reactions to A Woman Rabbi"
            (OBJF: 210-217)
            Ticktin: "A Modest Beginning" (TJW:
            129-138)

April 3 -   American Jewish Mythology: JAPS, JPS
            and Jewish Mothers
            Bart: "Portnoy's Mother's Complaint"
               (TJW: 72-83)
            Hyman: "The Jewish Family" (OBJF:
               19-26)
            Schneider: "Whom We Choose and Why"
               (JF: 287-317) and "Jewish Women in
               the Nuclear Family and Beyond" (JF:
               255-286)
            Monson: "The Case of the Reluctant
               Exogamists" (JF: 335-337)

April 10 - New Roles In Jewish Communal Affairs
            Cohen, et al.: "The Changing (?) Role
               of Women in Jewish Communal Affairs"
               (TJW: 193-201)
            Lipstadt: "Women and Power in the
               Federation" (OBJF: 152-166)
            Schneider: "Power and Participation in
               the Jewish Community" (JF: 445-474)

April 17 - New Life Cycle Rituals
            Leifer: "On The Birth of a Daughter"
               (TJW: 21-30)
            Koller-Fox: "Women and Jewish
               Education" (TJW: 31-42)
            Leifer: "On Writing New Ketubot" (TJW:
               50-62)
            Schneider: "Rhythms and Cycles" (JF:
               84-148)

April 24 - Students Talk About Their Papers
            Schneider: "Reconciling Jewish and
               Female" (JF: 84-148)

May 1 -   Students Talk About Their Papers and
            Synthesis

WOMEN AND JUDAISM

T. Drorah Setel
Harvard University

This one-semester undergraduate seminar met once a week
for three hours.

* * *

COURSE DESCRIPTION:

The seminar will focus on an analysis of Jewish women's
experience through the examination of specific issues.
We will study the Jewish woman through history from
biblical times to the present. Topics will include:
Women and the Bible, Women and Jewish Law, Women in
Sephardi Cultures, Women in Ashkenazi Cultures, Women
in modern Israel, and Jewish women in the contemporary
U.S. feminist movement and in contemporary Jewish
theology.

COURSE REQUIREMENTS:

In addition to weekly required readings, students will
be expected to report on recommended readings twice
during the semester, take an active part in class
discussion, and prepare a final research paper or
alternative project, to be arranged with the
Instructor.

The seminar will meet weekly during the term on
Thursday afternoon. We will also meet three additional
times: (1) for a Shabbat dinner on Friday 25 February--
time and place to be announced at the first seminar
meeting; (2) for a Rosh Chodesh (New Moon) celebration
on Tuesday 12 April; and (3) if possible, for a visit
to a ritual bath in the Boston area.

PLEASE NOTE:

Required course reading will be drawn mainly from:

Beck, Evelyn Torton, ed., Nice Jewish Girls (Persephone
    Press, 1982).

Christ, Carol P. and Judith Plaskow, eds., Womanspirit
    Rising (Harper & Row, 1979).

Koltun, Elizabeth, ed., The Jewish Woman (Schocken Books, 1976).

February 3   INTRODUCTION

February 10   BEGINNINGS: ORIGINS AND DEFINITIONS OF
                  JUDAISM, ORIGINS AND DEFINITIONS OF
                  PATRIARCHY

                  Required Reading:

                  Annette Daum, "Blaming Jews for the
                       Death of the Goddess," from Nice
                       Jewish Girls: A Lesbian Anthology,
                       Evelyn Torton Beck, ed. (Persephone
                       Press, 1982).

                  Carol Meyers, "The Roots of
                       Restriction," Biblical Archaeol-
                       ogist 41 (1978).

                  Judith Plaskow, "Blaming the Jews for
                       the Birth of Patriarchy," in Nice
                       Jewish Girls.

                  Merlin Stone, "When God Was a Woman,"
                       Womanspirit Rising, Christ, Carol
                       P. and Judith Plaskow, eds. (Harper
                       & Row, 1979).

                  Recommended Reading:

                  Kate Millet, Sexual Politics (Avon
                       Books, 1970), Chapter 1, part 2,
                       "Theory of Sexual Politics."

                  Rosemary Ruether, New Woman/New Earth
                       (Seabury Press, 1975), Chapter 1,
                       "The Descent of Woman."

                  Judith Ochshorn, The Female Experience
                       and the Nature of the Divine
                       (Indiana University Press, 1981),
                       Parts I and II.

                  Adrienne Rich, Of Woman Born (Bantam,
                       1977), Chapters III-IV.

February 17   WOMEN AND HEBREW BIBLE

Required Reading:

Genesis 1-3
Leviticus 19-20
The Song of Songs
The Book of Ruth

Claudia Camp, "The Wise Women of 2
    Samuel," Catholic Biblical Quar-
    terly.

Phyllis Trible, "Depatriarchalizing in
    Biblical Interpretation," from The
    Jewish Woman, Elizabeth Koltun, ed.
    (Schocken Books, 1976).

Recommended Reading:

David Bakan, And They Took Themselves
    Wives (Harper & Row, 1979), Chap-
    ters 3-7, 9.

Judith Ochshorn, The Female Experience,
    Part III and Epilogue.

Raphael Patai, The Hebrew Goddess (Avon
    Books, 1978), Introduction, Parts
    I, II, III.

Phyllis Trible, God and the Rhetoric of
    Sexuality (Fortress Press, 1978),
    Chapters 4, 6.

Arthur Waskow, Godwrestling (Schocken
    Books, 1978), Chapters I, V, VI,
    VII.

February 24   JEWISH LAW I: RABBINIC ATTITUDES AND
                  LEGISLATION

Required Reading:

Saul Berman, "The Status of Women in
    Halakhic Judaism," in The Jewish
    Woman.

69

Anne Goldfeld, "Women as Sources of
     Torah in the Rabbinic Tradition,"
     in The Jewish Woman.

Linda Kuzmack, "Aggadic Approaches to
     Biblical   Women,"   in   The   Jewish
     Woman.

Recommended Readings:

Louis Ginzberg, The Legends of the Jews
     (Jewish   Publication   Society   of
     America, 1911-38).

Blu Greenberg, "Jewish Women: Coming of
     Age," in On Women and Judaism
     (Jewish Publication Society, 1981).

Jacob Neusner, "From Scripture to
     Mishnah: The Origins of Mishnah's
     Division of Women," Journal   of
     Jewish Studies Vol. 30 (Fall 1979).

Judith Hauptmann, "Images of Women in
     the Talmud,"   in   Religion   and
     Sexism,   Rosemary   Ruether,   ed.
     (Simon and Schuster, 1974).

J.B. Segal, "The Jewish Attitude
     Towards Women," Journal of Jewish
     Studies Vol. 30 (Fall 1979).

Moses ben Maimon, The Code of
     Maimonides, Book Four: The Book of
     Women   (Yale   University   Press,
     1972), Treatise I: Chapters 1-4;
     10-21; 23-25.

Moses ben Maimon, The Code of
     Maimonides, Book Four
     Treatise II: Chapter 1; 10-13
     Treatise IV: Chapters 1-3
     Treatise V: Chapters 1-3.

March   3   WOMEN AND JEWISH LAW II: SEXUALITY

Required Reading:

Evelyn Torton Beck, "Why is This Book
     Different from All Other Books?" in
     Nice Jewish Girls.

Martha Shelley, "Affair With a Married
     Woman," in Nice Jewish Girls.

Rachel Adler, "Tumah and Taharah; Ends
     and Beginnings," in The   Jewish
     Women.

Recommended Reading:

Marcia Falk, trans., The Song of Songs
     (Harcourt Brace Jovanovich, 1973).

David Feldman, "The Positive Factors,"
     in Marital Relations, Birth Control
     and Abortion in Jewish Law
     (Schocken, 1974), Part 2.

Adrienne Rich, "Compulsory Heterosex-
     uality and Lesbian Existence," from
     Women: Sex and Sexuality (Uni-
     versity of Chicago Press, 1980),
     Stimpson, Catharine and Ethel
     Person, eds.

Maida Tilchen with Helen D. Weinstock,
     "Letters from My Aunt," in Nice
     Jewish Girls.

Arthur Waskow, Godwrestling, Chapter X.

March   10   WOMEN IN SEPHARDI CULTURES

Required Reading:

Savina Teubal, "A Coat of Many Colors,"
     in Nice Jewish Girls.

Rachel Wahba, "Some of Us are Arabic,"
     in Nice Jewish Girls.

71

Recommended Reading:

Marc D. Angel, "The Circle of Women," in
    The Jews of Rhodes (Sepher-Hermon
    Press, 1978), Chapter 7.

Sondra Henry and Emily Taitz, Written
    Out of History (Bloch Publishing,
    1978), Chapters V, VI, IX, X.

Cecil Roth, Dona Gracia of the House of
    Nasi (Jewish Publication Society,
    1974).

Cecil Roth, The Jews in the Renaissance
    (Harper & Row, 1965), Preface,
    Chapters I, II, III.

March   17   WOMEN IN ASHKENAZI CULTURES

Required Reading:

Gluckel of Hameln, The Memoirs of
    Gluckel of Hameln (Schocken Books,
    1977).

Recommended Reading:

Sondra Henry and Emily Taitz, Written
    Out of History, Chapters VII-VIII,
    XI-XIII.

Barbara Myerhoff, "Jewish Comes up from
    the Roots, in Number Our Days
    (Simon and Schuster, 1978), Chapter
    7.

Ruth Rubin, Voices of a People (McGraw
    Hill, 1973).

March   24   JEWISH WOMEN IN ISRAEL

Required Reading:

Evelyn Torton Beck, "Next Year in
    Jerusalem?" in Nice Jewish Girls.

Carol N. Clapsaddle, "Flight from
        Feminism: The Case of the Israeli
        Woman," in The Jewish Woman.

Marcia Freedman, "A Lesbian in the
        Promised Land," in Nice Jewish
        Girls.

Shelley Horwitz, "Letter from Jeru-
        salem,: in Nice Jewish Girls.

Recommended Reading:

Lesley Hazelton, Israeli Women: The
        Reality Behind the Myth (Simon and
        Schuster).

Rachel Katznelson Shazar, ed., The
        Plough Woman: Memoirs of the
        Pioneer Women of Israel (Herzl
        Press, 1975).

Natalie Rein, Daughters of Rachel:
        Women in Israel (Penguin Books,
        1980).

Hannah Senesh, "The Diary," and "The
        Letters," from Her Life and Diary
        (Schocken Books, 1971).

April   7   JEWISH WOMEN IN THE UNITED STATES

Required Reading:

JEB, "That's Funny, You Don't Look Like
        a Jewish Lesbian," in Nice Jewish
        Girls.

Irena Klepfisz, "Resisting and Surviving
        America," in Nice Jewish Girls.

Sonya Michel, "Mothers and Daughters in
        American Jewish Literature: The
        Rotted Cord," in The Jewish Woman.

Adrienne Rich, "Split at the Root," in
        Nice Jewish Girls.

Recommended Reading:

Charlotte Baum, Paula Hyman and Sonya
    Michel, The Jewish Woman in America
    (New American Library, 1975),
    Chapters 2-6.

Sondra Henry and Emily Taitz, Written
    Out of History, Chapter XIV.

David Philipson, ed., Letters of Rebecca
    Gratz (Jewish Publication Society,
    1929).

Anzia Yezierska, Red Ribbon on a White
    Horse (Persea Books, 1981).

April 12   ROSH CHODESH CELEBRATION

Required Reading:

Arlene Agus, "This Month is for You:
    Observing Rosh Hodesh as a Woman's
    Holiday," in The Jewish Woman.

Penelope Washbourne, "Becoming Woman:
    Menstruation as Spiritual
    Challenge," in Womanspirit Rising.

Recommended Reading:

Blu Greenberg, "In Defense of the
    'Daughters of Israel': Observa-
    tions on Niddah and Mikveh," in On
    Women and Judaism.

Rita Gross, Journal of the American
    Academy of Religion (Dec. 1977).

Marla Powers, "Menstruation and
    Reproduction," in Women: Sex and
    Sexuality.

April 14   U.S. JEWISH FEMINISM

Required Reading:

Laura Geller and Elizabeth Koltun,
    "Single and Jewish: Toward a New

Definition of Completeness," in The Jewish Woman.

Gloria Z. Greenfield, "Shedding," in Nice Jewish Girls.

Paula Hyman, "The Other Half: Women in the Jewish Tradition," in The Jewish Woman.

Irena Klepfisz, "Anti-Semitism in the Lesbian/Feminist Movement," in Nice Jewish Girls.

Aliza Maggid, "Lesbians in the International Movement of Lesbian/Gay Jews," in Nice Jewish Girls.

Recommended Reading:

Blu Greenberg, "Feminism: Is It Good for the Jews?," "Can A Mild-Mannered Yeshiva Girl Find Happiness among the Feminists?," "The Theoretical Basis of Women's Equality in Judaism," "Feminism and Jewish Survival," "Afterward," in On Women and Judaism.

Cherrie Moraga and Gloria Anzaldua, eds., This Bridge Called My Back (Persephone Press, 1981), "And When You Leave Take Your Pictures With You: Racism in the Women's Movement."

Lilith (Journal)

April   21   JEWISH FEMINIST SPIRITUALITY

Required Reading:

Aviva Cantor, "A Jewish Woman's Hagaddah," in Womanspirit Rising.

Naomi Janowitz and Maggie Wenig, "Sabbath Prayers for Women," in Womanspirit Rising.

Judith Plaskow, "Bringing a Daughter into the Covenant," "The Coming of Lilith," in <u>Womanspirit Rising</u>.

Judith Plaskow, "The Jewish Feminist: Conflict in Identities," in <u>The Jewish Woman</u>.

Recommended Reading:

Lynn Gottlieb, "The Secret Jew: An Oral Tradition of Women," <u>Conservative Judaism</u> 30 (1976).

<u>Response, A Contemporary Jewish Review</u>, Special Issue on Prayer, Nos. 41-42 (Fall-Winter, 1982).

Naomi R. Goldenberg, <u>Changing of the Gods</u> (Beacon Press, 1979), Chapters 1 and 2.

Blu Greenberg, "Women and Liturgy," in <u>On Women and Judaism</u>.

Judith Plaskow, "God and Feminism," <u>Menorah</u>, Vol. III, No. 2 (1982).

Arthur Waskow, "Spiraling Toward Messiah," and "Questions on the Path," in <u>Godwrestling</u>.

Carol Ochs, <u>Behind the Sex of God</u> (Beacon Press, 1977).

<u>Vetaher Libenu</u> (Sabbath Prayerbook; Congregation Beth El, Sudbury, MA, 1981).

Maggie Wenig and Naomi Janowitz, eds., <u>Siddur Nashim</u> (Providence, RI: Privately printed, 1981).

April   28   CONCLUSIONS

THE IMPLICATIONS OF FEMINISM FOR OUR JUDAISM

Margaret Moers Wenig
Hebrew Union College-Jewish Institute of Religion

This course is a successor to Professors Judith Plaskow and Eugene Borowitz' "Feminist Theories of Religion: The Implications for Judaism," which appeared in the first edition of this Guide. It is a one semester course which is offered in some form every other year to rabbinic and cantorial students. The class meets twice a week for 90 minutes.

* * *

In its Centenary Perspective, the CCAR boasts: "We... feel great satisfaction at how much of our pioneering conception of Judaism has been accepted by the Household of Israel. It now seems self-evident to most Jews: Feminism is among the most significant elements of modern culture..."

While Reform Judaism has, at least in principle, embraced the claims of "civil rights" feminism and proclaimed, "that women should have full rights to practice Judaism," it has only begun to respond to the more recent and radical claims of feminism that women's experiences and insights, neglected by Judaism, generate notions of ethics and spirituality quite different from those we know of as "Jewish."

This course is designed to expose you to the challenges and opportunities presented by recent feminism, to encourage you to articulate a personal response, to consider the implications for your Judaism and to formulate a creative synthesis.

Requirements:

1. Attendance in class and participation in class discussions. Sisterhood is a sine qua non of feminism. Similarly, commitment on the part of each member of this seminar to the other seminar members is a sine qua non of the course. In order to embark on this (sometimes perilous) spiritual journey each of us must consistently "be-there" for our fellow/sister travelers. It is argued by some feminists that theology ought to be a communal (rather than an individual) endeavor. While one may dispute this claim, this course will

place greater emphasis on the work of the group as a whole than on the work of individual seminar members. For that reason, class discussion is the most important element of this course. Auditors are welcome if and only if they too make a commitment to the group. Sporadic guests are not welcome unless a specific exception is made.

2. Completion of assigned readings prior to the class for which they are assigned. You will notice that most of the assigned readings were not written by Jews and do not deal directly with Judaism. The readings were chosen for their ability to stimulate us to think in fresh ways. It will be up to us to apply these new insights to our Judaism.

3. Preparation of one page of writing for each class session. The writing is a discipline intended to help you prepare for class. In most cases you will be asked for your thoughtful as well as subjective reactions to the reading. (Your reactions might include but not be limited to answers to the following questions: What in the reading rings true? What do you have difficulty understanding or accepting? What implications about Judaism can be drawn from this reading?) From time to time, when no reading has been assigned you will be asked to rely solely on your own memory and imagination. We will begin each class by reading outloud the brief pieces we have written (they need not be typewritten).

Schedule:

Tues. Feb. 12 - Introduction

I. Women's Experience and Women's Stories

Thurs. Feb. 14 - Women's stories as sacred texts
Read: Carol Christ, "Women's Stories, Women's Quest" in Diving Deep and Surfacing: Women Writers on Spiritual Quest (Beacon: Boston, 1980).

Tues. Feb. 19
Read: Rita Mae Brown, Rubyfruit Jungle, Alice Walker, The Color Purple.

78

Thurs. Feb. 21 - (Rosh Hodesh Adar)
     Read: Tillie Olsen, "I Stand Here Ironing," in
her Tell Me a Riddle.
     Flannery O'Connor, "The Life You Save May Be Your
Own" in her A Good Man is Hard to Find,
(Doubleday: New York, 1970).

Tues. Feb. 26 - On Mary Carmichael and Mary Shelley
     Read: Virginia Woolf, A Room of One's Own, Chap-
ters 4, 5, 6.
     Ellen Moers, "Female Gothic" (only pps. 90-99) in
her Literary Women, (New York: Doubleday, 1976).

Thurs. Feb. 28
     Telling our own stories about our mothers, grand-
mothers and surrogate mothers.

II. Women's Experiences and Feminist Ethics

Tues. Mar. 5 - Our own experience
     The Heinz Dilemma; real dilemmas we have faced

Thurs. Mar. 7 - (Purim)
     Read: Carol Gilligan, In a Different Voice:
Psychological Theory and Women's Development,
(Cambridge: Harvard Univ. Press, 1982).

Tues. Mar. 12 - The ethic of choice
     Read: Beverly Wildung Harrison, "Theology of
Pro-Choice: A Feminist Perspective," Parts I and
II in The Witness, Vol. 64, No. 7, July 1981 and
Vol. 64, No. 9, Sept. 1981.

Tues. Mar. 14 - Confronting the limits of our tradition
     Read: David Feldman, Marital Relations, Birth
Control and Abortion in Jewish Law, Part 5.

Tues. Mar. 19 - HUC-JIR Colloquium, no class

III. Women's Experience and Conceptions of God/Goddess

Thurs. Mar. 21 - All experiences of God/Goddess are
               mediated by language and culture.
     Read: Steven T. Katz, "Language, Epistemology,
and Mysticism" in his Mysticism and Philosophical
Analysis, (New York: Oxford, 1978).

Tues. Mar. 26 - Our Bodies Our Selves
Women's experiences: menstruation, sexuality,
preventing/planning conception, infertility,
pregnancy, miscarriage, childbirth, lactation,
weaning, child rearing, menopause, domestic vio-
lence, aging, rape, incest, abortion, love,
anger...

Thurs. Mar. 28 - The Personal is political, the poli-
tical is theological; Rape and the
Transcendent God as a Power Over us
Read: Susan Brownmiller, Against Our Will: Men,
Women and Rape, chapters 10 and 11.

Tues. April 2 - Our own preliminary statements about
God/Goddess

Thurs. April 4 - Implications of Goddess Worship
Read: Carol P. Christ. "Why Women Need the God-
dess: Phenomenological, Psychological and Poli-
tical Reflections" and Starhawk, "Witchcraft and
Women's Culture" both in Christ and Plaskow eds.
Womanspirit Rising: A Feminist Reader in
Religion, (San Francisco: Harper and Row, 1979)

Tues. April 9, Thurs. April 11 - Pesach, no class

IV. Feminist Theologies (From Radical to Reform) by
Daly, Ruether and Plaskow

Tues. April 16 - Introduction to Mary Daly, her move
from Liberation Theology to
Post-Christian Feminist Spirituality
Read: Mary Daly, Beyond God the Father: Toward a
Philosophy of Women's Liberation, (Boston: Beacon
Press, 1973), Introduction and Chapter 1.

Thurs. April 18 - (Yom Hashoa) Separatism, Lesbianism,
and the Liberation of Language
Read: Mary Daly, Gyn/Ecology: The Metaethics of
Radical Feminism, (Boston: Beacon, 1978)

Tues April 23
Read: Mary Daly, Pure Lust: Elemental Feminist
Philosophy, (Boston: Beacon, 1984)

Thurs. April 25 - Radical vs. Reform
Beverly Harrison's critique of Mary Daly; Where do
we stand?

Thurs. April 25 - Radical vs. Reform (cont.)
Beverly Harrison, "The Power of Anger in the Work of Love," in Making the Connections: Essays in Feminist Social Ethics. Edited by Carol S. Robb (Boston: Beacon Press, 1985).

Tues. April 30 - Christian Liberation Theology
Read: Rosemary Radford Ruether, Sexism and God-Talk: Toward a Feminist Theology, (Boston: Beacon Press, 1983), chapters 1-4.

Thurs. May 2
Read: Ruether, chapters 9-10 (to the end of the book).

Tues. May 7 - The Beginnings of A Jewish Feminist Theology
Read: Judith Plaskow, "The Coming of Lilith: Toward a Feminist Theology," in Plaskow and Christ, Womanspirit Rising: A Feminist Reader in Religion, (San Francisco: Harper and Row. 1979).

Thurs. May 9 - (Lag B'Omer)
Read: Judith Plaskow, "The Right Question is Theological," in Susannah Heschel ed., On Being A Jewish Feminist: A Reader, (New York: Schocken Books, 1983).

V.   Articulating a Feminist Critique of Liberal Judaism, a Liberal Jewish Critique of Feminism and a Synthesis of the Two

Tues. May 14 - Our Prayer Book and our Rituals (esp. Brit Milah and Havdalah)
Read: Rita Gross, "Female God Language in a Jewish Context," in Womanspirit Rising, and "Steps toward Feminine Imagery of the Deity in Jewish Theology," in On Being a Jewish Feminist.
Judith Plaskow, "Language, God and Liturgy: A Feminist Perspective," in Response, Vol., XIII, No. 4, Spring, 1983.

Thurs. May 16 - Our Institutions
Read: Adrienne Rich: "Toward a Woman Centered University," in her On Lies, Secrets and Silence: Selected Prose 1966-1978, (New York: Norton Press, 1979)

Tues. May 21 - (Rosh Hodesh Sivan) Our Thinkers:
        Cohen, Baeck, Kaplan, Rosenzweig, Buber
        (Heschel), and Borowitz
    Transcedent vs. immanent God/Goddess, is one more
    ethical?
    Is there a conflict between the principles of the
    autonomy of the individual and the ethic of
    relation?

Thurs. May 23 - Last Class, Personal statements of
        belief

THE JEWISH FAMILY IN HISTORY AND LITERATURE

Paula Hyman
Jewish Theological Seminary of America

This course was designed as an interdisciplinary synthesis course for rabbinical students to bring scholarship to bear on a broad subject of cultural concern. The course was structured to examine traditional prescriptive attitudes about marriage, sexuality, parenthood, the ideal male role and the ideal female role and to contrast those attitudes with the experiences of real Jewish families in a variety of social settings.

The class, which was first taught in the spring of 1985, was comprised of a few undergraduates, graduate students, and rabbinic students, and met once a week for two hours over a 13 week period. Professor Hyman notes that student response was positive, while female students were, on the whole, more enthusiastic about the course than were their male counterparts.

* * *

I.   Traditional Views of Jewish Family Life

Jan. 21   1.   Introduction and the Biblical Family

*Isaac Mendelsohn, "The Family in the Ancient Near East," Biblical Archaeologist Reader, Vol. 3, pp. 144-162.

*Roland de Vaux, Ancient Israel, Vol. 1, pp. 19-55.

Genesis, Chs. 16, 20, 24, 18
Deuteronomy, Ch. 24:1-4
Hosea, Ch. 2:21-22
Malachi, Ch. 2:14
Ezekiel, Ch. 16:8
Proverbs, Ch. 31:10-31

Jan. 28   2.   Rabbinic Attitudes--Marriage and Sexuality

*David M. Feldman, Marital Relations, Birth Control, and Abortion in Jewish Law, pp. 21-105.

Louis Epstein, <u>Sex Laws and Customs in Judaism</u>, pp. 104-131.

<u>Sefer Ha'Aggadah</u>, pp. 494-501.

Maimonides, <u>Mishneh Torah</u>, <u>Sefer Nashim</u>, Hilkhot Ishut, Ch. 12:1-6; 13:1-5, 8-18; 14:1-4, 8-11, 17-19; 15:1-3, 17, 19, 20; 16:1-4; 21:1-10. <u>Sefer Kedushah</u>, Hilkhot Issurei Viah, 21:5-12, 17-19, 21-23, 25-26; 22:1-2, 18-21.

Feb. 4 3. Rabbinic Attitudes--Parents and Children

<u>Sefer Ha'Aggadah</u>, pp. 494-501.

Maimonides, <u>Mishneh Torah</u>, <u>Sefer Shoftim</u>, Hilkhot Mamrim, 6:1-10, 12-14. <u>Sefer Nashim</u>, Hilkhot Ishut, 15:3-5; 19:1-2, 10-12, 16-17; 20:1-3, 21:16-18.

Feb. 11 4. Medieval Prescriptive Literature

*Israel Abrahams, <u>Hebrew Ethical Wills</u>, pp. 51-92, 127-161, 163-200, 207-218.

Nahmanides, <u>Iggeret Hakodesh</u>, Seymour J. Cohen, trans. & ed., pp. 40-43, 60-61, 66-67, 70-73, 78-81, 108-111, 114-117, 138-147.

II. The Traditional Jewish Family in its Settings

Feb. 25 5. In the Mediterranean World: The Geniza Sources

S.D. Goitein, <u>A Mediterranean Society</u>, Vol. III, pp. 1-248.

March 4 6. In Medieval Christendom

*Philippe Aries, <u>Centuries of Childhood</u>, pp. 15-49, 339-364.

Irving Agus, <u>Urban Civilization in Pre Crusade Europe</u>, Vol. 2, pp. 556-57, 568-69, 573-74, 588-89, 606-09, 620-21, 630-33, 638-46, 663-66, 668-71, 674-77, 682-88, 695, 697-705, 726-27.

Irving Agus, ed., <u>Rabbi Meir of Rothenberg</u>,
 pp. 280-83, 310-28, 330-35, 338-41,
 356-57, 378-81.

Recommended: Zeev Falk, <u>Jewish Matrimonial
 Law in the Middle Ages</u>.

March 11   7.   In Early Modern Europe: The Ashkenazi
 Family & its Community

*Jacob Katz, <u>Tradition and Crisis</u>, pp.
 135-56.

Katz, "Marriage and Sexual Life among the
 Jews at the End of the Middle Ages,"
 <u>Zion</u>, X (1944), pp. 21-54.

Herman Pollack, <u>Jewish Folkways in German
 Lands</u>, Chapter 2.

*<u>Memoirs of My People</u>, Leo W. Schwartz, ed.,
 pp. 103-114.

*Solomon Maimon, <u>An Autobiography</u>, pp. 15-34,
 101-04.

*<u>A Treasury of Jewish Letters</u>, F. Kobler,
 ed., Vol. 2, pp. 449-53, 456-58.

March 18   8.   From a Woman's Perspective

*<u>The Memoirs of Gluckel of Hameln</u>, Marvin
 Lowenthal, ed.

*<u>A Treasury of Jewish Letters</u>, Vol. 2, pp.
 364-67, 464-72.

III. The Impact of Modernity

March 25   9.   Emancipation and Mobility: Changing
 Roles for Men, Women and Children

Lawrence Stone, "Family History in the 1980s:
 Achievements and Future Trends," <u>Journal
 of Interdisciplinary History</u>, XII, i
 (Summer 1981).

*Pauline Wengeroff, "Memoirs of a
 Grandmother," in <u>The Golden Tradition</u>,
 Lucy Dawidowicz, ed., pp. 160-68.

Marion Kaplan, "Women and Tradition in the German Jewish Family," xerox, and "For Love or Money: The Marriage Strategies of Jews in Imperial Germany," Leo Baeck Institute Yearbook, XXVIII, 1983.

*Sholom Aleichem, "Hodel," in A Treasury of Yiddish Stories, Howe, Irving and Eliezer Greenberg, eds., pp. 168-82 or "Modern Children," in Selected Stories of Sholom Aleichem, pp. 229-248.

*William Toll, The Making of an Ethnic Middle Class, pp. 42-76.

April 1   10. The Immigrant Jewish Family in America

*A Bintel Brief, Isaac Metzker, ed., pp. 78-9, 86-7, 106-09, 156-58, 162-63.

*Irving Howe, World of Our Fathers, pp. 169-274.

*Baum, Hyman and Michel, The Jewish Woman in America, pp. 55-120, 187-233.

*Thomas Kessner, The Golden Door, pp. 71-103.

*Anzia Yezierska, "The Fat of the Land," in The Open Cage, pp. 77-104.

April 15   11. Reconstructing the Family: The Kibbutz

*The Plough Women, Rachel Katznelson Shazar, ed., pp. 145-49, 193-206.

Yonina Talmon, Family and Community in the Kibbutz, pp. 1-180.

April 22   12. The Contemporary Jewish Family in Israel

Calvin Goldscheider, "Family Change and Variation among Israeli Ethnic Groups," xerox.

Harold Greenberg, Israel: Social Problems, pp. 77-94.

Aharon Megged, "Yad Vashem," in Arba'ah
Sippurim, pp. 51-62. English
Translation: "The Name," in Israeli
Stories, Joel Blocker, ed., pp. 87-106.

April 29 13. The Contemporary Jewish Family in
America

Steven M. Cohen, "The American Jewish Family
Today," American Jewish Yearbook, Vol.
82 (1982), pp. 136-154.

*Philip Roth, Goodbye Columbus.

*Available in paperback

Requirements of the course:

Class participation
Final examination
A research paper or two interesting sermons

RELIGION AND HUMAN EXPERIENCE

Edward R. Zweiback Levenson
Villanova University

This undergraduate course has been offered periodically at Villanova since 1979. It is one semester in length, meeting 15 times, twice a week, for 75 minutes. Levenson notes that when Christ and Plaskow's Womanspirit Rising went out of print, he substituted Rosemary Radford Ruether's Sexism and God-Talk. He now uses Ruether's Womanguides as the primary text for women and/in religion.

* * *

Course objective:

To introduce, via lecture and discussion, a multi-dimensional interdisciplinary study of religion, in both its spiritual and corporate senses, as it has developed and been understood in modern history, influences society, and involves and reflects the individual personality.

Taking the five categories (natural science, biology, psychology, history, social theory) of the Johnson and Wallwork text, Critical Issues in Modern Religion, as structural guides, we shall analyze the life's work and viewpoints of the respective thinkers from Hume to Camara and Cone. Integrated in the readings are innovative contributions, in Womanspirit Rising, from the new feminist thought, which we shall discuss. The sensitive personal perspective of Michael Novak, in his Ascent of the Mountain, Flight of the Dove--a recommended text--will also interest you.

Texts:

Roger A. Johnson and Ernest Wallwork, with Clifford Green, H. Paul Santmire, and Harold Y. Vanderpool, Critical Issues in Modern Religion (Englewood Cliffs, NJ: Prentice-Hall, 1973).

Carol P. Christ and Judith Plaskow, eds., Womanspirit Rising: A Feminist Reader in Religion (NY: Harper and Row, 1979).

Michael Novak, <u>Ascent of the Mountain, Flight of</u>
   <u>the   Dove: An   Invitation   to   Religious</u>
   <u>Studies</u>, (NY: Harper and Row, 1971).

Requirements: Midterm examination - February 27

               Final examination

               A brief term paper (7-10 pages)
                  exploring a syllabus topic of your
                  choice and related reading. Due
                  April 11.

Week 1.   Introduction

               Reading:

               <u>Critical Issues</u>, pp. 1-9.

               <u>Womanspirit</u>, pp. 1-17.

               <u>Ascent</u>, <u>Flight</u>, pp. 1-42 (recommended).

Weeks 2, 3.   Natural Science and Religion

               David Hume: A Skeptic Examines
                  Religious Beliefs.
               Rudolf Bultmann: Beyond the Conflict
                  of Science and Religion--An
                  Existential Faith.

               Reading:

               <u>Critical Issues</u>, pp. 13-73.

Weeks 4, 5.   Biology and Religion

               Charles Darwin and Darwinism: A
                  Naturalized World and a Brutalized
                  Person?
               Pierre Teilhard de Chardin: The
                  Christianization of Evolution.

               The Essential Challenge: Does Theology
                  Speak to Women's Experience?

Reading:

Critical Issues, pp. 77-140.

Womanspirit, pp. 19-62.

Weeks 6, 7.   Psychology and Religion

Sigmund Freud: The Psychoanalytic
      Diagnosis--Infantile Illusion.
Dietrich Bonhoeffer: Religionless
      Christianity--Maturity,
      Transcendence, and Freedom.
Erik H. Erikson: Psychosocial Resources
      for Faith.

Reading:

Critical Issues, pp. 251-361.

Womanspirit, (Goldenberg on Dreams as
      Sources   of   Revelation),   pp.
      219-227.

Ascent, Flight (Autobiography and
      Story), pp. 43-87 (recommended).

Weeks 8, 9.   History and Religion

Ernst Troeltsch: Modern Historical
      Thought and the Challenge to
      Individual Religions.
Paul Tillich: The Relative and the
      Ultimate in the Encounter of
      Religions.
The Past: Does it Hold a Future for
      Women?

Reading:

Critical Issues, pp. 365-434.

Womanspirit, pp. 63-130.

Ascent, Flight (Cultures), pp. 88-115
      (recommended).

Weeks 10-12.   Social Theory and Religion

        Karl Marx: Religion--Social Narcotic
           and Reactionary Ideology.
        Reinhold Niebuhr: Religion Fosters
           Social   Criticism   and   Promotes
           Social Justice.
        Religious Radicals: Camara and Cone:
           Christians in the Revolution of the
           Oppressed.

        Reading:

        Critical Issues, pp. 143-247.

        Ascent, Flight (Societies, Institutions,
           Organizations), pp. 117-197 (recom-
           mended).

Weeks 13, 14.   The Emergence of Post-Modern Religion.
        Summary.

        Reconstructing Tradition; Creating New
        Traditions.

        Reading:

        Critical Issues, Epilogue, pp. 435-459.

        Womanspirit, pp. 131-218, 228-287.

        Ascent, Flight (Nature and History), pp.
           198-209 (recommended).

FEMINIST THOUGHT AND WESTERN RELIGION: CONFLICTS, COMPROMISES, & CONSEQUENCES

Faith Rogow
State University of New York at Binghamton

This was taught as a four week summer course, and met every day for two hours. Because it was a summer course, it was conducted with a relaxed, small seminar format that encouraged participation by all class members. The seminar format and the emphasis on reading primary texts made it easy for the instructor to tailor discussions for beginning or more advanced students. Faith Rogow writes, "My favorite aspect of this course is that it emphasizes teaching students how to ask more concise questions rather than memorize static answers."

* * *

The primary goals of this course are (1) to learn how to learn from one another; (2) to learn how to ask historical questions; and (3) to examine:

a. What happens when strong Judeo-Christian traditions which have been guiding the Western world for centuries are confronted by feminism, which seeks to change the direction of that path?

b. How have women been affected and viewed by Western religions?

c. How has feminist thought been influenced by and reacted to Judeo-Christian tradition?

Our emphasis will be to compare responses of the authors we read and of class members.

FORMAT: The first half of class will be lecture with interrupting questions. The second half will be called "Working It Through" (WIT). In this section the class will work through a text or an issue together. Occasionally this second section will require individual reports.

REQUIREMENTS: Because we will concentrate on learning as a group, class participation will

constitute 50% of the grade. Participation is defined as: regular attendance, preparing class readings, and
completing all assignments ON TIME.

Another 25% of the grade will be based on
a 2 page book review or a 5 page topical
study. Books and topics must be approved
by the instructor. Several articles by
the same author may be substituted for a
book.

A comprehensive final (I.D. & essay) will
be worth the remaining 25%.

TEXTS: (All texts will be on reserve. Students
are advised to purchase only those texts
which are used frequently.)

The Bible - any translation which includes the Old & New
     Testaments and the Apocrypha is O.K.
(WR) Womanspirit Rising - Carol Christ and Judith
     Plaskow, eds.
(PWS) The Politics Of Women's Spirituality - Charlene
     Spretnak, ed.
The Woman's Bible - Elizabeth Cady Stanton
The Jewish Woman - Elizabeth Koltun, ed.
Biblical Affirmations Of Woman - Leonard Swidler
Religion & Sexism - Rosemary Ruether, ed.
Women Of Spirit - Rosemary Ruether
New Woman, New Earth - Rosemary Ruether
Women and Religion in America - Rosemary Ruether &
Rosemary Keller, eds.
Response magazine, Summer 1973
A variety of thought provoking articles...

1.   INTRODUCTION

2.   THE ROLE OF RELIGION IN WESTERN CULTURE

          WR: Preface, Saiving, pp. 25-42

          WIT: Religion in American pop culture vs.
          separation of Church and state.

3.   JUDAISM ON WOMEN: A STUDY IN AMBIVALENCE

          Swidler, pp. 71-160
          Adler, Hyman & Hauptman in Response

Hauptman & Bird in Religion & Sexism
Hyman & Berman in The Jewish Woman

WIT: "Woman of Valor" - Proverbs 31

Assignment: Choose a religious woman from the Middle Ages and prepare a 2 page biographical sketch. Due in class #9.

4. CHRISTIANITY ON WOMEN: JESUS AS FEMINIST?

Swidler, pp. 161-336
WR: Fiorenza, pp. 84-92

5. TEXT READING: PAUL, THE CREATION STORY, LILITH

Genesis 1 & 2
WR: Plaskow, pp. 198-209
Trible, pp. 74-83 or Trible in The Jewish Woman

6. THE MATRIARCHS AND THE POWER OF WRITING

Genesis - all

WIT: The "Binding of Isaac": A Modern Midrash (copies will be handed out in class).

Assignment: Write 3 discussion questions based on readings for next class. Due next class.

7. BIBLICAL HEROES: ARE THEY FEMINIST?

Bible: Esther, Judith, Susannah, Judges 4 & 5

WIT: Developing discussion questions.

8. THE VIRGIN MARY, FEMALE SAINTS, & THE SHEKHINAH

New Woman, New Earth - Chapter 2
WR: Pagesis, pp. 107-120

9. PERSONALITIES: RELIGIOUS WOMEN IN THE MIDDLE AGES

WIT: Exchanging reports: Is there a common denominator?

Assignment: Each student will be assigned a passage from Stanton's Woman's Bible. Be prepared

94

to present and discuss your assigned passage. Due class #11.

10.   WOMEN IN THE CLERGY/WOMEN IN EVANGELICAL MOVEMENTS

Ruether (71-98), McLaughlin (99-130), Liebowitz (131-152) in Women of Spirit: Women and Religion in America, pp. 1-45

WIT: Nancy Cott's "Religion and the Bonds of Womanhood," in Our American Sisters (Friedman & Shade, eds.)

11.   THE FEMINIZATION OF AMERICAN RELIGION
(Lecture should include the work of Ann Douglas and Barbara Welter, though they are not included in the required reading.)

Women and Religion in America - Introduction Mary Maples Dunn's "Women of Light," in Women of America: A History (Berkin & Norton, eds.)

12.   CAN YOU BE A FEMINIST IN A PATRIARCHAL RELIGION?

WR: McLaughlin, pp. 93-106
Introductions to Mary Daly's The Church and the Second Sex, Beyond God the Father, and Gyn/Ecology

WIT: The development of Mary Daly: feminist theology in progress.

13.   RESPONSE: CHANGE FROM WITHIN

WR: pp. 174-192
Any two articles from The Jewish Woman
New Woman, New Earth - chapter 3

14.   MATRIARCHIES AND THE GREAT MOTHER

PWS: Stone (7-21), Adler (127-137)
WR: Stone, pp. 120-130

15.   FEMINIST PROPOSALS FOR THE FUTURE: THE GODDESS

WR: Christ (273-287) or PWS (71-86)
Audre Lorde's "An Open Letter to Mary Daly," in This Bridge Called My Back, (Moraga & Anzaldua, eds.)

WIT: Recognizing racism in our visions.

BOOK REVIEWS DUE

16. WITCHES

New Woman, New Earth, Chapter 4
WR: Starhawk, pp. 259-268

17. THE POLITICS OF WOMEN'S SPIRITUALITY

Each student will be assigned an article from
PWS.

WIT: Presenting book reviews - sharing our
work.

18. FEMINISM AND THE MORAL MAJORITY

Each student should watch and be prepared to
report on a television evangelical show and
how they present women.

19. RELIGION IN WOMEN'S MUSIC & HUMOR

(Presentation will include political cartoons,
cartoons from M.S. Maronek's With Love to
Father Church, and music from a variety of
sources, including Izquierda, Sweet Honey in
the Rock, Kay Gardner, Davida Ishatova, and
Maxine Feldman.)

WIT: Review

20. FINAL EXAM

BIBLIOGRAPHY

Christ, Carol and Plaskow, Judith, eds. Womanspirit
    Rising: A Feminist Reader in Religion. San
    Francisco: Harper & Row, 1979.

Cott, Nancy. "Religion and the Bonds of Womanhood," in
    Friedman, Jean E. and William G. Shade, eds. Our
    American Sisters. Boston: Allyn & Bacon, 1976.

Daly, Mary. Beyond God the Father. Boston: Beacon
    Press, 1973.

    The Church and the Second Sex. NY: Harper & Row,
    1975.

    Gyn/Ecology: The Metaethics of Radical
    Feminism. Boston: Beacon Press, 1978.

Douglas, Ann. The Feminization of American Culture.
    NY: Avon Books, 1978.

Dunn, Mary Maples, "Women of Light," in Berkin, Carol
    Ruth and Mary Beth Norton, eds. Women of America:
    A History. Boston: Houghton Mifflin, 1979.

Koltun, Elizabeth, ed. The Jewish Woman: New
    Perspectives. NY: Schocken, 1976.

Lorde, Audre, "An Open Letter to Mary Daly," in Moraga,
    Cherie and Gloria Anzaldua, eds. This Bridge
    Called My Back. Watertown, MA: Persephone Press,
    1981.

Response: A Contemporary Jewish Review. No. 18, Summer
    1973.

Ruether, Rosemary Radford. New Woman, New Earth:
    Sexist Ideologies and Human Liberation. NY:
    Seabury Press, 1975.

    Women of Spirit: Female Leadership in the Jewish
    and Christian Traditions. NY: Simon & Schuster,
    1979.

    Religion and Sexism: Images of Women in the Jewish
    and Christian Traditions. NY: Simon & Schuster,
    1974.

with Rosemary Skinner Keller, eds. Women And
Religion in America, Vol. 1. San Francisco:
Harper & Row, 1981.

Spretnak, Charlene, ed. The Politics of Women's
Spirituality. Garden City, NY: Anchor Books,
1982.

Stanton, Elizabeth Cady. The Woman's Bible. Reprint
NY: Arno Press, 1972 [c. 1895].

Swidler, Leonard. Biblical Affirmations of Woman.
Philadelphia: Westminster Press, 1979.

Welter, Barbara. Dimity Convictions. Athens, OH: Ohio
University Press, 1976.

AMERICAN JEWISH EXPERIENCE

Maxine S. Seller
State University of New York at Buffalo

This course is an updated version of Seller's course that appeared in the first edition of the Guide. It is an undergraduate course taught bi-annually for one semester. Class meetings are held twice a week for 90 minutes.

* * *

Required texts:

Henry Feingold, A Midrash on American Jewish History
Charlotte Baum, Paula Hyman, Sonya Michel, The Jewish
    Woman in America
Marc Lee Raphael, ed., Jews and Judaism in the United
    States
Anzia Yezierska, Breadgivers

Course requirements:

1. A midsemester and a final exam.

2. Reading assignments as indicated below.

3. At least one written and oral presentation of a book listed under the weekly "options". The student should spend 15-20 minutes in class describing the content of the book, relating the book to the required reading of the week, and raising questions for class discussion. The presentation must be during the appropriate week and a written summary (3-5 pages) must be handed in at least one class before the oral presentation. To obtain an "A" for the course, the student must present two options (although two presentations will not guarantee an "A" if other work is not excellent).

1. Jan. 22, 24   Introduction

    Feingold, Preface, ix-xv.
    Abraham Karp, "Jewish Perceptions of America,"
        (handout).
    Jacob Rader Marcus, Early American Jewry, Vol. 1,
        pp. 3-23.

2. Jan. 29, 31   Colonial Beginnings

    Feingold, pp. 1-25.
    Baum, ch. 1.
    J.R. Marcus, <u>The American Jewish Woman: A
        Documentary History</u>, pp. 1-5, 28-31, 32-35,
        42-46, 67.
    Richard Morris, "The Role of Jews in the American
        Revolution," from <u>Jewish Life in America</u>,
        Gladys Rosen, pp. 8-27.

3. Feb. 5, 7   Men and Women from Germany

    Feingold, ch. 2, pp. 27-54.
    Raphael, pp. 33-45 (Economic and Social Life, the
        19th Century).
    Moshe Davis, <u>The Emergence of Conservative
        Judaism</u>, pp. 65-78 ("The Changing Communal
        Order").
    Baum, ch. 2.
    Marcus, <u>The American Jewish Woman</u>, pp. 170-177,
        204-222, 135-143, 306-314.

    <u>Options</u>:

    Bertram Korn, <u>German Jewish Intellectual
    Influences in America</u>, <u>Jews and the Civil War</u>, <u>The
    American Reaction to th Mortara Case</u>; Hyman
    Grinstein, <u>The Rise of the Jewish Community of New
    York 1654-1860</u>; Stephen Birmingham, <u>Our Crowd</u>;
    Leon Harris, <u>Merchant Princes</u>; Alexander Lee
    Levin, <u>The Szolds of Lombard Street</u>; Rebecca
    Kohut, <u>My Portion</u>; Annie Nathan Meyer, <u>It's Been
    Fun</u>; Hannah Solomon, <u>Fabric of My Life</u>.

4. Feb. 12   Anti-Semitism in 19th and early
                   20th century America.

    Guest lecturer, Professor David Gerber.

    Raphael, pp. 251-297. (No class Feb. 14.)

5. Feb. 21   Religious Reform

    Feingold, pp. 56-68.
    Marcus, <u>The American Jewish Woman</u>, pp. 286-288,
        292-300.
    Raphael, pp. 185-205.

Options:

James Heller, Isaac Mayer Wise; I.M. Wise, Reminiscences; W. Gunther Plaut, The Growth of Reform Judaism, A Historical Perspective; L. Jick, The Americanization of the Synagogue.

6.   Feb. 26, 28   Newcomers from Eastern Europe

Baum, ch. 3 and 4.
Feingold, pp. 69-82.
Irving Howe, World of Our Fathers, pp. 5-46.
Raphael, pp. 47-66.

Options:

Mark Zbrowski and Elizabeth Herzog, Life is With People; Ruth Rubin, Voices of a People: The Story of Yiddish Folksong; Jonathan Sarna (trans. and ed.), People Walk on Their Heads: Joseph Weinberger's Jews and Judaism in New York; Ande Manners, Poor Cousins; Thomas Kessner, The Golden Door: Italian and Jewish Immigrant Mobility in New York City; G. Davidson, Our Jewish Farmers and the Story of the Jewish Agricultural Society; Sydelle Kramer and Jenny Masur, Jewish Grandmothers.

7.   March 5   Buffalo's Jews (Guest lecturer,
                   Professor Mark Goldman.)

       March 7   Midsemester examination

8.   March 12, 14   Yiddish Culture: Theatre and Music

Feingold, pp. 83-93.
Hutchins Hapgood, Spirit of the Ghetto, ch. 5,
    "The Stage."
Mark Slobin, Tenement Songs: The Popular Music of
    the Jewish Immigrants, ch. 6, pp.
    119-163.
(Classroom "workshop" performance of a one act Yiddish play--in English translation, March 14.)

Options:

Nahma Sandrow, Vagabond Stars; Lulla Rosenfeld, Bright Star of Exile: Jacob Adler and the Yiddish Theatre; David Lifson, Yiddish Theatre in America; Mark Slobin, Tenement Songs.

9.   March 19, 21   Yiddish Culture: Press and
                      Literature

      Hutchins Hapgood, Spirit of the Ghetto, ch. 6,
          "The Press," and ch. 7, "The Sketch
          Writers."
      Norma Fain Pratt, "Culture and Radical Politics:
          Yiddish Women Writers 1890-1940," American
          Jewish History, LXX: 1 (Sept. 1980), pp.
          68-89.

      Options:

      Robert E. Park, The Immigrant Press and Its
      Control; Charles Madison, Yiddish Literature;
      Anzia Yezierska, Hungry Hearts; Max Rosenfeld, A
      Union for Shabbos.

10.   March 26, 28   Secular Ideologies: The Labor
                      Movement and Zionism

      Feingold, pp. 94-108.
      Baum, ch. 5.
      Seller, Immigrant Women, "In Memoriam--American
          Democracy" (Emma Goldman), pp. 259-264.
      Irving Howe, World of Our Fathers, pp. 204-208.
      Raphael, "American Zionist Organization," pp.
          125-137.

      Options:

      H. Hurvitz, The Workman's Circle; L. Glen Seretan,
      Daniel De Leon: The Odyssey of An American
      Marxist; Emma Goldman, Living My Life and
      Anarchism and Other Essays; Rose Zeitlin,
      Henrietta Szold; Melvin Urofsky, American Zionism
      from Herzl to the Holocaust; Leon Stein, The
      Triangle Fire.

11.   April 9, 11   Organization and Americanization

      Yezierska, Breadgivers.
      Baum, ch. 6, 7.
      Feingold, pp. 110-125.
      Raphael, pp. 11-125, 137-153 (American Jewish
          Committee, American Jewish Congress,
          Anti-Defamation League).

Options:

A. Cahan, The Rise of David Levinsky; Henry Roth, Call It Sleep; Scholom Asch, East River; Naomi Cohen, Not Free to Desist (American Jewish Committee); Arthur Goren, New York Jews and the Quest for Community: The Kehillah Experiment; Morton Rosenstock, Louis Marshall, Defender of the Faith.

12. April 16, 18   "At Home in America?" 1920-1940

Irving Howe, "The East European Jew in American
    Culture," in Rosen, Jewish Life in America,
    pp. 92-108.
Feingold, pp. 127-139 (The Conservative Movement);
    pp. 177-191 (anti-semitism in the 1920's).
Raphael, pp. 67-92 (Jews in the economy); pp.
    213-233 (The Conservative and Reconstruc-
    tionist Movements); pp. 278-303 (anti-
    semitism).
Norma Fain Pratt, "Transitions in Judaism: The
    American Jewish Woman through the 1930's,"
    American Quarterly, 1979, p. 681.

Options:

John Higham, Strangers in the Land; S. Steinberg, The Academic Meltingpot; William Toll, The Making of an Ethnic Middle Class: Portland Jewry over Four Generations; Leonard Dinnerstein, Anti-semitism in the United States; Deborah Dash Moore, At Home in America: Second Generation Jews; Mordecai Kaplan, Judaism as a Civilization; Marshall Sklare, Conservative Judaism: An American Religious Movement.

13. April 23, 25   The Holocaust and the State of
                    Israel

Feingold, ch. IX, pp. 141-159 and ch. XII
    and XIII, pp. 193-220.
Raphael, pp. 319-329 (The anti-Nazi boycott);
    316-318 (the "Holocaust Hoax").

Options:

Yehuda Bauer, The Holocaust in Historical Perspective; Henry Feingold, The Politics of Rescue: The

Roosevelt Administration and the Holocaust; S.
Halprin, The Political World of American Zionism;
Arthur Morse, While Six Million Died; Marshall
Sklare, The Impact of Israel on American Jewry;
Melvin Urofsky, We Are One: American Jewry and
Israel; Dorothy Rabinowitz, New Lives; Jacob
Neusner, Strangers At Home: The Holocaust,
Zionism, and American Jewry.

14. April 30 and   Changing Lifestyles and
     May 2   Institutions

     Eli Ginzberg, "The Dynamics of Opportunity," in
          Gladys Rosen, Jewish Life in America, pp.
          109-119.
     Baum, ch. 8.
     Anne Lerner, "Who Hast Not Made Me a Man: The
          Movement for Equal Rights for Women in
          American Jewry," American Jewish Yearbook,
          1977.
     Feingold, pp. 160-176 (revitalization of
          Orthodoxy); 221-234 (Can American Jewry
          Survive?).
     Raphael, pp. 153-162 (United Jewish Appeal,
          philanthropy); 208-213 (Reform Platform of
          1976. Compare to Pittsburgh Platform of 1887
          on pp. 203-205); 237-247 (Haverot--
          alternative Judaism).
     "The Philistine Philanthropists: The Power and
          Shame of Jewish Federations," in Peter Dreier
          and Jack Porter, Jewish Radicalism.

     Options:

     Abraham Lavender, ed., A Coat of Many Colors:
     Jewish Subcommunities in the United States; D.
     Rabinowitz, The Other Jews: Portraits in Poverty;
     David Sidorsky, The Future of the Jewish Community
     in America; Elizabeth Koltun, ed., The Jewish
     Woman; G. Scholem, On Jews and Judaism in Crisis.

15. May 7   Jews and Other Americans

     Gladys Rosen, Jewish Life in America:
          M. Konvitz, "The Quest for Equality," pp.
          28-56.
          Marshall Sklare, "Jewish Acculturation," pp.
          167-188.
          Ronald Berman, "Some Notes from the Third
          Generation."

Raphael, pp. 304-316, 329-335 (Jews and Blacks).

Options:

Meier Kahane, The Story of the Jewish Defense League; Mordecai Chertoff, The New Left and the Jews; Stephen Isaacs, Jews and American Politics; Susan Welch and Fred Ullrich, The Political Life of American Jewish women.

WOMEN AND RELIGION

Celia Y. Weisman
Barnard College

Celia Weisman has been teaching this course at Barnard College since the spring of 1980, and writes that "the course remains always exciting and fresh, since each year new students bring new and familiar issues and problems to the classroom." Her description of the course continues.

I invite my students to respond to the material we study together in a "wholistic" way. Though this term may sound a trifle glib to our jaded mid-80s ears, I encourage an educational approach that seeks to integrate mind and spirit, body and soul, idea and intuition. In other words, I hope to teach feminist process as well as content. Thus the term "wholistic" does adequately describe the pedagogical model I utilize. Although I don't allow class time to slip into a rap session mode, the atmosphere in this class is casual, supportive and friendly. Inevitably the class turns itself into a cohesive community, even though students come from a wide variety of religious backgrounds and levels of observance.

I usually speak for about one-third of each class period, and the rest of our time is occupied with discussion and in-class writing exercises.

The course structure resembles that of a spiral; we pick up certain ideas, examine them and let them go, only to return to them later, in different contexts. This spiraling movement is repeated several times throughout the semester, so students begin to recognize thematic parallels which cut across the different cultural traditions we investigate.

Student response has been extremely favorable. When I first offered the course in 1980 I had a grand total of sixteen students; in the spring of 1985, fifty-two women and four brave young men showed up regularly to attend the class. The syllabus has been very successful; students love the combination of history, fiction, philosophy and theology that it contains. They also enjoy the openness of the final assignment. Over the years, many have opted to keep semester-long journals as their final projects, and have found this to be an enriching and rewarding experience.

The class meets for sixteen weeks, for two sessions a week, each lasting 75 minutes.

* * *

Course Requirements:

1. Reading of assigned materials, participation in discussion, and periodic short writing exercises. Regular class attendance at class sessions is extremely important.

2. A take-home midterm paper to be prepared in 2 weeks.
   Assignment distributed: March 7th
   due: March 21st

3. A final project. The project can be a paper, or a creative composition, or a journal. If students opt to fulfill this requirement by keeping a journal, they must begin recording their thoughts, observations, images, dreams, visions, reading notes, and quotations on women and religion in a bound volume early in the term. Journals will also be looked at by the instructor at least once before midterm.

The following books are available at the Columbia Bookstore. All books and articles needed for the course are also on reserve in Barnard Library.

ASSIGNED TEXTS:

Andrews, Lynn. Medicine Woman. (San Francisco: Harper and Row) 1981.
Christ, Carol P. and Judith Plaskow, eds. Womanspirit Rising. (San Francisco: Harper and Row) 1979.
Gordon, Mary. The Company of Women. (New York: Random House) 1980.
Gornick, Vivian and Barbara K. Moran, Woman in Sexist Society. (New York: New American Library) 1971.
Heschel, Susannah, ed. On Being a Jewish Feminist. (New York: Schocken Books) 1983.
Niethammer, Carolyn. Daughters of the Earth. (New York: MacMillan) 1977.
Rosaldo, Michelle Zimbalist and Louise Lamphere, eds. Women, Culture and Society. (Stanford: Stanford University Press) 1974.

Shange, Ntozake. For Colored Girls Who Have Considered
Suicide When the Rainbow is Enuf. (New York:
MacMillan) 1977.
Spretnak, Charlene, ed. The Politics of Women's
Spirituality. (New York: Anchor Books) 1982.
Summers, R bv. Montague, trans. of Heinrich Kramer's
and James Sprengers' The Malleus Maleficarum.
(New York: Clover Publications, Inc.) 1971.
Walker, Alice. The Color Purple. (New York: Pocket
Books) 1982.

TOPICS AND READINGS:

I.   Introduction / Jan. 24 -- 29

        Sherry Ortner, "Is Female to Male as Nature is to
           Culture," in Rosaldo and Lamphere, eds.,
           Woman, Culture and Society, pp. 67-88.
        Vivian Gornick, "Woman as Outsider," in Woman in
           Sexist Society, pp. 126-144.

II.   Native American Traditions / Jan. 31, Feb. 5, 7

        Lynn V. Andrews, Medicine Woman
        Caroline Niethammer, Daughters of the Earth, pp.
           37-57, 235-249.

III.   Women and Judaism / Feb. 12, 14, 19, 21, 26

        The Bible, Revised Standard Version
           Selections
        Phyllis Bird, "Images of Women in the Old
           Testament," in Ruether, ed., Religion and
           Sexism, pp. 41-88.
        Judith Hauptmann, "Images of Women in the Talmud,"
           in Ruether, pp. 184-212.
        Susannah Heschel, On Being a Jewish Feminist

IV.   Women and Christianity / Feb. 28, March 5, 7,
                                         19, 21

        The Bible, RSV, selections
        Constance Parvey, "The Theology and Leadership of
           Women in the New Testament," Ruether, pp.
           117-149.
        Elaine Pagels, "What Became of God the Mother?,"
           in Carol P. Christ and Judith Plaskow, eds.,
           Womanspirit Rising, pp. 107-119.

Eleanor Commo McLaughlin, "Equality of Souls, Inequality of Sexes: Women in Medieval Theology," in Ruether, pp. 213-266.
Jane Dempsey Douglass, "Women and the Continental Reformation," in Ruether, pp. 292-313.
Mary Gordon, The Company of Women

V. Goddess Studies and Feminist Theology /
                         March 26, 28, April 2

Merlin Stone, "The Great Goddess: Who Was She?," in Spretnak, pp. 7-21.
Carol P. Christ, "Why Women Need the Goddess: Phenomenological, Psychological and Political Reflections," Spretnak, pp. 71-86.
Mary Daly, "Gyn/Ecology: Spinning New Time/ Space," Spretnak, pp. 207-212.
Kay Turner, "Contemporary Feminist Rituals," Spretnak, pp. 219-233.

VI. Witchcraft / April 4, 9, 11

Margaret A. Murray, The Witchcult in Western Europe, pp. 9-27.
Jacob Sprenger and Heinrich Kramer, Malleus Maleficarum,
    p. 96 Begin with ch. 1 up to p. 101 "A Few Points..."
    p. 118 Begin with ch. VII -- p. 119.
    p. 213 Begin with Question VII up to p. 214 Question VIII
    p. 222 Begin with Question XIII up to p. 225 Question XIV
Starhawk, "Witchcraft as Goddess Religion," Spretnak, pp. 49-56.
Naomi Goldenberg, "Feminist Witchcraft: Controlling Our Own Inner Space," Spretnak, pp. 213-218.

VII. Black Women and Spiritual Quest / April 16, 18,
                                           23, 25

Ntozake Shange, For Colored Girls
Sabrina Sojourner, "From the House of Yemanja: The Goddess Heritage of Black Women," Spretnak, pp. 57-63.
Alice Walker, The Color Purple

VIII. Summary and Conclusion / April 30

    Presentation of Projects

            * * *

Regarding language ...

Please attempt to use non-genderized language in class
and written work. This is sometimes tricky, but is
easier than you might think. Substitute humankind for
mankind. Repeat "God" rather than write "He." Use
"her or his" or "his or her" or "s/he." Be
inventive!!!

A book which might be helpful in this area is:

Casey Miller and Kate Swift, The Handbook of Nonsexist
    Writing for Writers, Editors and Speakers. New
    York: Lippincott and Crowell

RESOURCES:

The Women's Center
100 Barnard Hall
Monday through Friday, 9-5
Women's studies library; subscriptions to feminist
    periodicals

Womanbooks
92nd Street and Amsterdam Avenue
873-4121
Feminist bookstore

Union Theological Seminary
Broadway and 120th Street
662-7100
Theological library and bookstore; women's center

Jewish Women's Resource Center
9 East 69th Street
535-5900
Library, resources, Rosh Hodesh gatherings

New York Feminist Art Institute
325 Spring Street
242-1342
Workshops and events on women's art and spirituality

SOURCES FOR FEMINIST SPIRITUALITY:
LISTENING TO WOMEN'S VOICES

Sue Levi Elwell
National Havurah Summer Institute

This course was offered during a five-day adult study
Institute during the summer of 1985. The class met for
four seventy-five minute sessions. Each day's discussions were based on the readings as outlined below.

* * *

READINGS

1. Adrienne Rich, "Transcendental Etude," The Dream
   of a Common Language: Poems 1974-1977 (NY:
   W.W. Norton & Co., 1978), pp. 76-77.

2. Carter Heyward, "Our Efforts to be Whole/healed,"
   from Our Passion for Justice: Images of
   Power, Sexuality, and Liberation (New York:
   The Pilgrim Press, 1984), pp. 168-170.

3. Cynthia Ozick, "Torah as the Matrix for Feminism,"
   in Lilith 12/13, pp. 47-48.

4. Pauline Wengeroff, "Memoirs of a Grandmother,"
   from The Golden Tradition: Jewish Life and
   Thought in Eastern Europe, Lucy Dawidowicz,
   ed. (Boston: Beacon Press, 1967), pp.
   160-168.

5. Sarah Schenirer, "Mother of the Beth Jacob
   Schools," in Dawidowicz, pp. 206-209.

6. Puah Rakowski, "A Mind of My Own," in Dawidowicz,
   pp. 388-393.

7. Three Tkhines translated by Tracy Guren Klirs from
   "Bizkhus fun Sore, Rivke, Rokhl un Leye: The
   Tkhine as the Jewish Woman's Self-
   Expression." Unpublished rabbinic thesis,
   Hebrew Union College-Jewish Institute of
   Religion, 1984.

8. Excerpts from Etty Hillesum's An Interrupted Life
   (New York: Pantheon Books, 1983), pp. 45,
   46, 52, 61, 72-3, 78, 113, 114, 115, 131,
   146-7, 158, 173-4, 191-2, 194, 205.

9.   Merle Feld, "Sinai" (unpublished poem).

10.   Ona Siporin, "<u>Mikveh Mayim</u>: Becoming a Jew," <u>The Jewish Calendar 5746</u> (New York: Universe Books, 1985).

11.   Linda Stern Zisquit, "Posit" (unpublished poem).

12.   Lynn Gottlieb, "Speaking into the Silence," <u>Response</u> 41/42 (Fall 1982).

13.   Esther Broner, "The Song of Questions," <u>A Women's Haggadah</u>
      "The Women's Commandments," <u>A Weave of Women</u>
      (New York: Holt, Rinehart and Winston, 1978), pp. 280-281.

14.   Merle Feld, "We All Stood Together" (unpublished poem).

CREATING MIDRASH

Irene Fine
Woman's Institute for Continuing Jewish Education

In 1977 the Woman's Institute for Continuing Jewish Education began, and I thought it entirely possible that we would be in existence for only one year. I planned to teach one course each quarter for three quarters. Given this limited amount of time, I asked myself, "What materials are absolutely essential for women to discover their roles in Jewish History?" My answer was a history course (World of Our Mothers) in fall, a ceremony course (Mothers, Daughters, Sisters and Jewish Rites of Passage) in winter, and a literature course (A Woman's Eye view of Jewish Fairy Tales-- the title was later changed to simply: Creating Midrash) in spring.

The Institute has survived for nine years and "Creating Midrash" has been my favorite. While teaching this course I discovered the importance of not only "midrashic" process (see below) but also the learning process of the women themselves, the internal changes within learners as they begin to create in history. Watching women grow in self-esteem and achievement as they master a Jewish "tool" or craft still provides me with a profound sense of accomplishment and wonder.

The Institute's classes are usually held once a week for six weeks, and the enrollment in creative classes is small, most often six to ten people. The enthusiasm and persistence of the people electing to learn midrash compensates for the small enrollment and there are very few drop-outs. The first session entitled "Introduction" is one I use at conferences with anywhere from 50 to 100 people attending.

During the first class session my biggest job may be helping the learner overcome her basic resistance to creating Jewish history. This resistance is usually demonstrated by the "do I know enough?" syndrome. This question usually results from lack of involvement in creative work in other Jewish learning situations. As a teacher my first responsibility is to put everyone at ease, and I usually do this by pointing out that the first midrashim came from "folk" or people like themselves who enjoyed telling the stories and giving oral explanations which updated ancient material for their own generations. Another way of overcoming resistance

is for the class to create the first midrashim together, collectively, by brainstorming ideas.
Subsequent midrashim can be developed at home.

The classes last an hour and a half (7:30-9:00 p.m.)
and have two parts. The first 45 minutes is spent
reading and analyzing Torah, rabbinic midrashim and
modern midrashim. The next 45 minutes is again divided
between listening to original midrashim by learners,
commenting on them, and then setting the mood for the
new creative work which will follow during the week.
One time, in class, I had women hold their compact
mirrors up to the text and tell me what new meaning
they envisioned reflected back.

Women are encouraged to start using their new midrashim
as soon as possible within their community setting. In
the past midrashim has been included in life cycle
ceremonies such as adult bat mitzvah and midlife ceremonies, shared with family after candle lighting on
Friday nights and incorporated into Havurah services.

COURSE DESCRIPTION

The tradition of creating midrash is an ancient one.
From the time of Ezra the Scribe (5th C. BCE) until the
present, people have invented fresh, new interpretations of biblical themes. These brief explanations, or
midrashim, keep alive biblical themes and help build a
bridge between past and present.

Women are becoming more involved in the midrashic
process, the steps which guide them toward creating
midrashim. This course will involve the learner in
this process which is briefly to: 1) read the Torah,
2) search the literature for midrashim already explain-
ing the passage, and 3) create new midrashim which
explain the passage in light of woman's experiences.

The modern midrashim used in class are selected because
they are imaginative, descriptive and reflect either
women's issues or women as protagonists. Learners are
encouraged to bring to class other midrashim they find
during their first week's readings that can be used for
class discussion.

The objective of the class is for each learner to
create and present to the class at least three original
midrashim.

COURSE LENGTH: Six, one and a half hour sessions.

REQUIRED READING: Taking the Fruit: Modern Women's
                   Tales of the Bible

COURSE OUTLINE:

I.   Introduction: The history of midrash and
     explanation of midrashic process.

               Taking the Fruit, pp. 3-14 and 11, 28
               Genesis 1:26-27 and 2:18-24
               Marc Gellman, "Partners" and "The First
                  People"
               Ginzberg, Legends of the Jews, p. 66

II. Creation:

               Midrash Rabbah, Vol. 1, pp. 2-14
               Genesis 1-2:24
               Legends of the Jews, pp. 3-29
               Educating the New Jewish Woman, pp.
                  99-102
               "A Midrash" in Blessing the Birth of a
                  Daughter, p. 116

III.   Confrontation:
         Jewish Woman New Perspectives, pp. 11-17
         Educating the New Jewish Woman, p. 90
         Genesis 30:8   Speiser, pp. 230-231
         Taking the Fruit, pp. 36-37

IV. Characterization:

               Genesis 19:26   Taking the Fruit, pp.
                                     32-33
               Exodus 1:17-19   Taking the Fruit, pp.
                                     42-43

V.   Liberation:

               Back to the Sources, pp. 201-203
               Passover Haggadah "The Four Sons"
               San Diego Women's Haggadah, Second
                  Edition, pp. 24-26

VI. Siyyum and presentation of original
     midrashim.

115

Bibliography:

Bin Gorion, Micha Joseph. <u>Mimekor Yisrael</u>.
    Bloomington: Indiana University Press, 1976.
Christ, Carol P. <u>Diving Deep and Surfacing</u>. Boston:
    Beacon Press, 1980.
Fine, Irene. <u>Developing a Jewish Studies Program for</u>
    <u>Women: A Springboard to History</u>. Doctoral
    Dissertation. Ann Arbor: University Microfilms
    International, 1981.
Fine, Irene. <u>Educating the New Jewish Woman, A Dynamic</u>
    <u>Approach</u>. San Diego: Woman's Institute for
    Continuing Jewish Education, 1985.
Freedman, Rabbi Dr. H. and Maurice Simon, eds. <u>The</u>
    <u>Midrash Rabbah</u>. London: Soncino Press, 1977.
Gellman, Marc. "The First People," <u>Moment</u>, October
    1977.
Gellman, Marc. "Partners," <u>Moment</u>, January-February,
    1978.
    (ed. note: Only two of the many modern midrashim
    Marc Gellman has written which can be found in
    issues of <u>Moment</u> magazine.)
Ginzberg, Louis. <u>The Legends of the Jews</u>. Phila-
    delphia: The Jewish Publication Society of
    America, 1937.
Goldenberg, Naomi. <u>Changing of the Gods</u>. Boston:
    Beacon Press, 1979.
Grumet, Elinor. "Day Six, Day Seven," <u>Moment</u>, June
    1980.
Holtz, Barry, ed. <u>Back to the Sources: Reading the</u>
    <u>Classic Jewish Texts</u>. New York: Summit Books,
    1984.
Koltun, Elizabeth, ed. <u>The Jewish Woman--New</u>
    <u>Perspectives</u>. New York: Schocken Books, 1976.
Leviant, Curt. <u>Masterpieces of Hebrew Literature</u>. New
    York: KTAV Publishing House, Inc., 1969.
Patai, Raphael. <u>Gates to the Old City</u>. New York:
    Avon Books, 1980.
Schwartz, Howard. <u>Gates to the New City</u>. New York:
    Avon Books, 1983.
Speiser, E. A. <u>Genesis</u>. New York: Doubleday and
    Company, Inc., 1964.
Strack, Hermann L. <u>Introduction to the Talmud and</u>
    <u>Midrash</u>. New York: Atheneum, 1978.
Strassfeld, Sharon and Michael. "A Midrash." In Toby
    Reifman, ed. <u>Blessing the Birth of a Daughter</u>.
    New Jersey: Ezrat Nashim, 1977.
Zones, Jane Sprague. <u>San Diego Women's Haggadah,</u>
    <u>Second Edition</u>. San Diego, Woman's Institute for
    Continuing Jewish Education, 1986.

WORLD OF OUR MOTHERS: JEWISH WOMEN AND YIDDISH LITERATURE

Sharon Kleinbaum
National Yiddish Book Center

This non-credit course was sponsored by the National Yiddish Book Center in Amherst, Massachusetts, and was taught by Kleinbaum when she was assistant director of the Center. The class met once a week for eight 2 1/2 hour sessions. Many of the class participants were unaffiliated Jews who represented a wide range of professional and social commitments. Response to the course was very positive, and led several participants to continue their explorations in Yiddish literature and Jewish history.

* * *

1. Introduction to Traditional Eastern European Jewish Society.

   Readings:

   Irving Howe, World of Our Fathers (NY: Simon and Schuster, 1976) Chapter 1, "Origins."
   Mark Zborowski and Elizabeth Herzog, Life is With People (NY: Schocken Books, 1962), Prologue, "Road to the Shtetl."
   Abraham J. Heschel, "The Eastern European Era in Jewish History," in Voices From the Yiddish, Irving Howe, ed. (Ann Arbor: University of Michigan Press, 1972).

2. Traditional Role of Women and the Traditional Role of Yiddish; Early Yiddish Writings: A Literature for women and "men who are like women."

   Readings:

   Irving Howe and Eliezer Greenberg, A Treasury of Yiddish Stories (NY: Schocken, 1973), pp. 19-25.
   The Memoirs of Gluckel of Hameln (NY: Schocken Books, 1977).
   "Tsenerene: The Creation of Jacob Ben Isaac Ashkenazi," in The Shtetl, Joachim Neugroschel, ed. (NY: Perigee Books, 1979).

117

"Woe to the Father Whose Children are Girls:
Women in the Jewish Tradition," in Baum,
Hyman and Michel, The Jewish Woman in America
(NY: New American Library, 1976).

Short Story:

Abraham Reisen, "The Kaddish," in Yiddish Tales,
Helena Frank, trans. (Philadelphia: Jewish
Publication Society, 1912).

3.   Di yidishe froi, dos yidishe vaybel, dos yidishe
meydel (The Jewish woman, the Jewish wife, the
Jewish Girl).

Readings:

Charlotte Baum, "What made Yetta Work: Economic
Role of Eastern European Jewish Women in the
Family," in Response: The Jewish Woman
(Summer 1973, #18).
Baum, Hyman and Michel, Chapter 3.

Short Stories::

Y.L. Peretz, "A Woman's Fury," in The Shtetl,
Joachim Neugroschel (NY: Perigee Books,
1979).
"Devotion Without End," in Treasury
of Yiddish Stories, Irving Howe and Eliezer
Greenberg, eds. (NY: Schocken, 1973).
Shalom Asch, "A Scholar's Mother," in Yiddish
Tales.
"A Jewish Child," in Yiddish Tales.
Sholem Aleichem, "Gymnasye," in Yiddish Tales.

4.   Jewish Wives and Mothers

Readings:

"Women and the Shtetl Patriarchy: Dawn of a New
Social Consciousness," in Women of the Shtetl:
Y.L. Peretz, Ruth Adler (NJ: Fairleigh
Dickinson University Press, 1980).

Short Stories::

Y.L. Peretz, "An Idyllic Home," in Peretz, Sol
Liptzin, ed. and trans. (NY: YIVO, 1947).

5.　　Daughters

　　Readings:

Sholem Aleichem, <u>Tevye's Daughters</u>, Frances
　　Butwin, trans. (NY: Crown, 1949).
"Sholem Aleichem's 'Tevye Stories': The Crisis of
　　Family Life" in <u>From Shtetl to Suburbia</u>,　Sol
　　Gittleman (Boston:　Beacon Press, 1978).

6.　　Women in Non-traditional Roles

　　Readings:

Norma Fain Pratt, "Culture and Radical Politics:
　　Yiddish Women　Writers, 1980-1940," <u>American
　　Jewish History</u>, Sept. 1980.
Baum, Hyman and Michel, Chapter 5, "Weaving the
　　Fabric of　Unionism:　Jewish　Women Move　the
　　Movement."
Evelyn Beck, "Teaching About Jewish Lesbians in
　　Literature,"　in　<u>Lesbian　Studies</u>,　Margaret
　　Cruikshank, ed.　(NY:　The　Feminist　Press,
　　1982).

7.　　Yiddish Women Writers

　　Readings:

Norma Fain Pratt, "Anna Margolin's <u>Lider</u>:　A
　　Study in Women's　History, Autobiography　and
　　Poetry,"　in　<u>Studies　in　American　Jewish
　　Literature</u> (Albany:　SUNY Press, 1983) #3.
Irving Howe, <u>A Treasury of Yiddish Poetry</u> (NY:
　　Schocken　Books,　1976).　Poetry　of　Celia
　　Dropkin, Kadia　Moldowsky,　Rachel　Korn　and
　　Anna Margolin. We read the Yiddish originals
　　in class also.)
Ruth Rubin, <u>Voices of a People:　Yiddish Folksong</u>
　　(Philadelphia:　Jewish　Publication　Society,
　　1979).
Esther Kreitman, <u>Deborah</u>, Maurice Carr, trans.
　　(London:　Virago Press, 1983).

8.　　Anzia Yezierska (native Yiddish speaker who wrote
　　in English) And the　Struggle　to adjust　to　<u>Di
　　Goldene Medine</u>

Readings:

Baum, Hyman and Michel, "They Made a Life:
    East European Jewish Women in America,"
    Chapter 4.
Anzia Yezierska, The Open Cage (NY: Persea
    Books, 1979).
    "The   Fat   of   the   Land,"   "The   Lost
    Beautifulness," "America and I," "Children of
    Loneliness."
    The Bread Givers (NY: Persea Press, 1975).

THE JEWISH WOMAN IN FACT AND FICTION

Marcia Cohn Spiegel
University of Judaism

* * *

Introduction:

This class was designed for the Women's League of the Conservative Movement. It was part of a series on women's studies at the University of Judaism Department of Continuing Education and has also been taught in a modified form for synagogue and center classes, and organization retreats and workshops. While as many as 45 women have taken this class at one time, the ideal class size is 12 to 20 to maximize the participation of each member. This curriculum followed an intensive examination of the women of the Bible, which ended with a discussion of "The Woman of Valor" and the kind of model which that presents for Jewish women. That is a good place to begin this series. The selections were made to facilitate reading aloud at the time of class discussion, because many of my adult education students choose not to do outside reading. Discussion technique followed the rules for Great Books groups, with only a minimum of historical information, the discussion being focused on what women had to say about their own lives and the world in which they lived. The excitement of this class is the extent to which the participants became immersed in the process of discovery. As they read the words of the women who preceded them and try to create an image of a real person in another time and place, they illuminate their own world and put their own lives into a new perspective.

Course Description:

Throughout Jewish history we have been a people on the move--from a place where things were not going well to a place where we hoped our lives would be better. Usually the head of the family initiated the move and the rest of the family followed along, as Sarai followed Avram, Rachel and Leah moved with Jacob, and our mothers before them packed and schlepped and started over in a new place, in a new language, in a new culture. These moves created family tension as shifts occurred in economic class and status, family roles and responsibilities, language, customs, and even

121

in religious observance. In periods of economic prosperity some women were freed from domestic responsibilities and had the opportunity for both education and leisure. What remains of the works of women is from those times when women were literate, and the Jewish community itself more settled or prosperous. These selections reveal the extent to which the writers were dependent on their families and community attitudes for their own survival and esteem.

The purpose of this course is to help students reclaim the history of Jewish women by reading their words and interpreting historical source material. The instructor provides only that historical information necessary to understand the time and place in which the document was written. The student becomes the scholar as she seeks the clues that reveal the women beneath: Who is she? How does she feel about herself? What are her relationships to her family and to the world outside of her family? In order to fully understand the work a consideration is also given to the language in which it is written and why it was written in that language, and of course to consider if the woman herself wrote it, or if it was written for her.

Discussion of the historical documents should explore the meaning of each particular document and what it reveals about the roles and status of both women and Jews in that particular society. The reader becomes a detective, searching for the clues that unravel the mystery. The instructor is only a guide to give the required background information, keep the discussion moving and to point the class in a new direction.

An additional spiritual dimension was provided by reading the poetry of women of the period from a dramatic reading, The Jewish Woman: A Portrait in Hew Own Words by Marcia Cohn Spiegel (NY: National Federation of Temple Sisterhoods, 1976). A collection of women's prayers will be available after Winter, 1986, Women Speak to God: The Prayers of Jewish Women Through the Ages, edited by Marcia Cohn Spiegel and Deborah Lipton Kremsdorf (San Diego, CA: The Women's Institute for Continuing Jewish Education).

Course Length:

Two semesters. One two to two and a half hour discussion each week. There are three separate sections in this course. Each may be given as a separate class or workshop.

Part I: The Years of Wandering

The Woman of Valor
    Proverbs 31

Women of the Talmud

>   Beruriah and Ima Shalom
>   Sondra Henry and Emily Taitz, Written Out of History: Our Jewish Foremothers (Fresh Meadows, NY: Biblio Press, 1983), pp. 44-48.

Letters from Cairo Geniza
    Henry and Taitz, pp. 76-82.

13th Century:

>   The Jewess Who Became a Catholic
>   Jacob Rader Marcus, The Jew in the Medieval World (NY: Atheneum, 1975, pp. 142-144.

14th Century:

>   Family Connections
>
>   Henry and Taitz, pp. 102-107.

15th Century:

>   Sumptuary Laws
>   Marcus, pp. 194-196.

16th Century:

>   From Mother to Son
>   Franz Kobler, Letters to Jews Through the Ages: Biblical Times to the Middle of the 18th Century (Philadelphia: Jewish Publication Society, 1978), pp. 364-367.

>   From Rebbetzin Mizrachi
>   Henry and Taitz, pp. 108-113.

>   The Prayers of Rebecca Tiktiner
>   Henry and Taitz, pp. 92-100.

A Jewish Beautician to the Court of the Sforzas
     Marcus, pp. 399-400.

Sarah Copia Sullam, Cultural Leader of the
Venetian Ghetto
     Kobler, pp. 436-448.

17th Century:

     Ten Commandments for the Jewish Married Woman
          Marcus, pp. 443-444.

     Letters from Prague
          Henry and Taitz, pp. 152-169.

     A Gentile Seeks to Force a Jewess into Marriage
          Marcus, pp. 459-460.

     Gluckel of Hameln
          The Memoirs of Gluckel of Hameln (NY:
          Schocken Books, 1977). The following
          sections:

          Book Two, Section One   pp. 23-26.
          Book Two, Section Three   32-38.
          Book Three, Section Three   47-56.
          Book Three, Section Ten   86-89.
          Book Four, Section Fourteen   136-142.
          Book Five, Section Two and Three 152-155.
          Book Six, Section One and Two   222-227.
          Book Seven, Section One and Two   254-257.
          Book Seven, Section Seven   264-267.

18th Century:

     Rachel Varnhagen: Assimilation in the Salons
          Hannah Arendt, Rachel Varnhagen: The Life of
          a Jewish Woman (NY: Harcourt, Brace,
          Jovanovich, 1974), pp. 56-58, 80-86, 118-127,
          193-196, 220-223.

19th Century:

     Letters from America, Assimilation in
     the Colonies
          Jacob Rader Marcus, American Jewish Woman: A
          Documentary History (NY: KTAV, 1981), pp.
          14-20, 28-31, 42-45, 68-71, 170-177, 260-267,
          329-334.

20th Century:

Going Home: Settling the Land of Israel
    Rachel Katznelson Shazar, The Plough Woman
    (NY: Herzl Press, 1975), pp. 27-32, 43-50,
    89-93, 105-110, 137-144, 193-200, 209-211.

The Holocaust: Death and Survival
    Etty Hillesum, An Interrupted Life   (NY:
    Pantheon Books, 1983), the following journal
    entries or letters:

June 8 and 14, 1941	pp. 22-25.
August 4	27-31.
	33-34.
August 26	36.
October 20	44-46.
February 27, 1942	71-73.
	76-77.
April 26 to May 30	104-115.
June 29	127.
July 3	130-141.
July 14	152-153.
July 28	164-165.
September 22	177-178.
August 24, 1943	207-223.

These selections were reprinted in Moment
Magazine (December, 1983, Volume 9, #1).

Frida Michelson, I Survived Rumbuli (NY:
Holocaust Library, 1979), pp. 68-9, 74-84,
162-171, 195-198, 225-232.

At the concluding class for Part I participants should
bring in memorabilia, letters, diaries, journals,
ethical wills which belonged to the women in their
families. Pictures and handicrafts, even recipes may
evoke the women who preceded them. This is a technique
to integrate family memories into the historical
context.

Part II: Coming to America

In a new home, whether it was Venice, Minsk, Samarkand
or New York City, a predictable cycle began. The
parents who initiated the move felt displaced and
uncomfortable. They had to learn to function in a new
environment, while their children grew up in the new
culture, with a different language and life style.
Some women went to work and adapted to the new life as
they strove to provide for their families, others
stayed at home raising small children excluded from the
changes taking place around them. For a period of
several generations the differences in these life
styles caused conflicts and misunderstandings between
parents and children. A woman's sense of her own
self-esteem is forged within the parameters established
by these differences.

The following selections were chosen to explore the
process of change that took place in the movement from
Europe to America at the turn of this century. They
explore the differences and expectations of a
generation of immigrant women, and the conflicts
between family members because of these differences.
In discussing the selections from Lillian Hellman's
memoirs, it is important to remember that this is a
Southern Jewish family that was already thoroughly
assimilated when they were confronted with political
reality of the 20th century as it is played out in
their own family.

Not all of the following selections start at the top
of the page noted. The readings relate to inter-
generational relationships, interfamilial conflicts and
differences, feelings about being Jewish and feelings
about being American.

Mary Antin, <u>The Promised Land</u> (Boston: Houghton
    Mifflin, 1912), pp. 32-37, 48-59, 68-71, 244-251.

Anzia Yezierska, <u>Bread Givers</u> (NY: Doubleday, 1925,
    reprinted by Persea Books, 1975), pp. 1-23,
    173-184, 237-241.

Ruth Rosen and Sue Davidson, <u>The Mamie Papers: The
    Letters of Mamie Pinzer to Fanny Quincy Howe</u> (Old
    Westbury, NY: Feminist Press, 1977), pp. 25-26,
    34-37, 50-55, 104-105, 158-167, 192-198, 247-253,
    268-272, 398-400.

Isaac Metzker, A Bintel Brief (NY: Ballantine Books, 1971), pp. 32-34, 39-42, 63-65, 117-118, 136-137, 142-143, 155-156, 166-168, 171-171, 180-181, 186-188.

Isaac Metzker, A Bintel Brief, Vol. II (NY: Viking Press, 1981), pp. 27, 34-37, 120-122, 132-133.

Lillian Hellman, Pentimento (NY: Signet Books, 1973), pp. 5-39, 125-172.

Joanne Greenberg (Hannah Green), I Never Promised You a Rose Garden (NY: Holt, Rinehart, Winston, 1964), pp. 9-14, 16-17, 29048, 146-148, 236, 244-250.

Susan Fromberg Schaeffer, Falling (NY: Avon/Bard, 1973), pp. 3-9, 20-23, 44-57, 65-77.

Erica Jong, Fear of Flying (NY: Signet Books, 1973), pp. 21, 31-2, 38-46, 53-57, 59-61, 80-81, 114-115, 147-154.

Part III: Exploration and Reconciliation

While we each get a sense of our selves from our mothers we often forget that they in turn were influenced by their mothers. Many of us had better relationships with our grandmothers than with our mothers, forgetting that the tensions that exist between mothers and daughters existed for them too. It is hoped that by the end of this session we will have a deeper understanding of the women who helped to shape our lives, to understand their options, to be compassionate for their limitations, and to see how these have created our own self-esteem, options and limitations. From this new perspective we may be moved to make changes in our lives and to reach across the generations with a new bond of strength and love.

In the communities from which they came, the economy was probably on a downward spiral; Jews who may once have been successful were struggling to survive, pushed by forces of politics and economics beyond their control. In the community to which they moved, the economy was probably beginning an upward cycle; there were places at the bottom from which to rise. But the starting point was the bottom. Combined with all the other pressures was the added loss of self-esteem of the parents' generation, magnifying even further the differences between parents and children.

Other factors impinged on the lives of the women. In a world of shifting values and economy, frustration, anger and disorientation may lead to behaviors that are disruptive and even violent. The Jewish concept of Shalom Bayit (Peace in the Home) created an ideal which families tried to emulate. But sometimes it was only an ideal--the reality may have been quite different, even unbearable. In an assimilating society these behaviors were kept "under wraps," concealed from the world outside, and the women suffered in silence. There were women who were without families, widows raising their children along, deserted wives unable to remarry, unmarriageable girls, women in same sex relationships, handicapped girls and prostitutes. There were women of great courage who carried on despite anything; who raised their children and held families together in the worst of times.

The history of each of our lives is made up of all of these facets. We are a reflection of all that went before. Each of our lives is unique; there are no stereotypes here.

Structure of Workshop

If the class is large, it can be divided into workable smaller units of six to eight people. Make sure that there is ample space for these groups to meet in smaller sessions and then reconvene to share the results of the small group discussions. If it is impossible to break the group into small units the exercises may be done by having each person share with one other person (the women sitting next to her for example).

While this workshop is planned for women only, it also works for mixed groups of men and women. Most men have never examined these issues, and find it enlightening to understand not only their mothers and grandmothers, but also the other women in their lives.

Because each group is different, a variety of exercises is suggested. No more than three can be done in a two hour workshop that allows for ample discussion. The exercises are arranged in such a way that you may select the most appropriate ones for your group. The workshop can be a minimum of two hours, or may be arranged as an all day program, a series of classes or even a weekend retreat.

No time limit is suggested for any single activity since the factors that influence the time for each exercise include the number of people in the group, the number of small groups needed and the amount of discussion that takes place during the general sharing. It is wise to allow at least 45 minutes for each exercise. However, at one retreat I conducted we started introducing ourselves by telling a little about our grandmothers, mothers and ourselves, and the participants found the variety of experiences so involving that we spent most of the workshop sharing just that information.

The leader should establish the rules:

>We are not to place value judgments on other people's experiences.

>We are describing, not judging.

>We must allow each participant to express her own feelings without fear of criticism.

>Each person is to speak only once until everyone has had a chance, then she may share other thoughts.

>We will then be open to the variety and diversity of the lives of others.

The facilitator's role is to introduce the exercise, explain the rules, make sure that each participant has an opportunity to talk, reconvene the group for open discussion and sharing following the small group sessions, and to keep the discussions focused. She should be sensitive to nuances of the group's feelings. She should summarize the discussion so that each exercise has a closure that provides a sense of what was discovered.

Each workshop should consist of:

>1. An opening statement utilizing the introductory remarks to Part III and an outline of the planned activities.

>2. A get-acquainted exercise.

3.   One exercise which explores the grandmother, the mother and the individual.

4.   And finally a ceremonial closing which offers an opportunity for reconciliation.

Beginnings

Some women may not know anything about their past, for their mothers or grandmothers may have been killed in the Holocaust. Others who are converts or the children of converts may feel uncomfortable at this point because of their differences from the group. The leader should be sensitive to these issues to help these women feel part of the group and to share as much of their past as they are able. If they can only remember their paternal grandmother then that is the one they should focus on, realizing that it will change their understanding of their mother's development. If they have no knowledge of their family history, they may want to recreate one, using women whom they know something about. Since the purpose is to gain insight into our own feelings, anything that works is fine.

1.   Getting to Know You. Each participant can wear a nametag which gives some historical or factual piece of information about her:

    a.   In mobile urban communities it is interesting to learn where people have come from and when they moved there.

    b.   The birthplaces of their grandmother, their mother and themselves can be listed.

    c.   What year their grandmother, mother (or even earlier great-grandmother) came to this country. List the first woman in the family to come to the U.S., where they came from, where they first settled.

Even women who are good friends do not usually know these details about each other.

2.   ZAKOR (remembrance). Because for many of us there is no written history of our immediate family, each participant is asked to bring a family object which has significance to her. This can be something that belonged to the women in the family and may include prayerbooks,

130

candlesticks, needlework, clothing, cooking utensils, etc.

As an introductory exercise, the women should be paired off, preferably with someone they don't know well, and each given a number: 1 or 2. First, #1 tells her partner #2 about the object that she brought and its significance to her for two minutes. Next #2 tells her partner #1 about her object. (No more than two minutes each for this--use a whistle or bell to indicate the time.) Finally with the group in a circle have each woman introduce her partner to the group, and tell something about the object her partner brought for about 30 seconds.

This exercise not only gives each woman a chance to bond with her partner, it will set an underlying emotional tone for the rest of the exercise.*[1]

3. <u>Pair and Share</u>. An alternate exercise is to have the women pair off and relate briefly the history of geographic movement in their family, going back as far as they can go. Follow the rules for <u>ZAKOR</u>, but allow for three to five minutes each. As the members go around introducing their partners, the leader should write down the information on each woman as follows:

Great-grandmother	Grandmother	Mother	Self
Where born? When? When?	Where? When?	Where? When?	Where?
Moved to?	Moved to	Moved to	Moved to

4. <u>Who am I? Pair and Share</u>. Following the rules for <u>ZAKOR</u> each partner describes herself in 1 1/2 minutes. Her name and the various roles she plays in her life.

The first exercise should focus on getting people acquainted with each other, with the group and to sense a connectedness to the past.

Exploring our Pasts

The following exercises are the core of the program. One or more may be chosen. Allow ample time to explore each question and the feelings they arouse. The facilitator should encourage openness. She should be prepared for some people who will hold back at first, particularly when there are painful memories. Others will rush in and try to control the discussion with their own stories. Gentle tact is needed to encourage one and to discourage the other. The insights gained during the workshop are triggered by these exercises: the sharing of our stories and our feelings about the women involved.

1.   <u>Changing Landscapes, Changing Values</u>. Leaders should post signs in various parts of the room. Each of the signs has one of the following statements.

>   BORN AND RAISED OUTSIDE OF THE UNITED STATES
>   BORN OUTSIDE OF THE U.S., RAISED IN U.S.
>   1ST GENERATION BORN IN U.S.
>   2ND OR LATER GENERATION BORN IN U.S.

Ask the participants to go to the corner with the appropriate sign for her grandmother. After sharing information about where the grandmother lived discuss the primary values of the grandmother--was it to achieve (A) Economic success, (B) Survival of the Jewish People, (C) Happiness and/or self-fulfillment. Each person should take a minute or two to reply; following their response one person from each group should share with the whole the consensus of the group. The leader should point out similarities and differences between the groups. Were values related to where and when the women were born? How did they change?

Next repeat the exercise for the mother. Finally for the participant. If the people in the group have daughters they might want to do it for their daughters. After each movement, the leader should explore the trends and distinctions that come up, and make a concluding summary statement.*[2]

2.   <u>Journey to the Past</u>. In groups of 6 to 8, have women close their eyes while the leader gets them comfortable, relaxed and takes them on a fantasy trip to their grandmother's kitchen:

132

"You are six years old, sitting in your grandmother's kitchen. You are sharing a glass of tea. She is telling you about her life. She is describing what she does and how she feels about herself. She tells you what is bothering her. She tells you what gives her pleasure. What is she telling you?"

When the participants have had an opportunity to share some of their story (to limit the time I suggest that they only share with their original partner), repeat the exercise with their mother. Again the leader should help them to relax:

"You are a little girl in your mother's kitchen. You are drinking a glass of milk while your mother tells you about her life, how she feels about herself. What is she complaining about? What makes her smile?"

After the participants have shared with at least one other person, the leader should collect the following information on a large paper, by a show of hands only--no discussion.

What education did their grandmothers have?
Primary? Secondary? College?
Professional? Religious?
How many had grandmothers who worked?
What jobs? Inside the home or outside?
Did they work for money or personal
gratification?
Were they fulfilled in their roles or did
they find it demeaning?
Were they frustrated in their roles? Were
they happy?

Repeat the questions about the mother. This exercise is designed to help put their lives into perspective, recognizing the goals, values, and opportunities available to these women. It is not unusual to find a group where very few grandmothers or mothers worked outside the home, nor is it unusual to find groups where most of them worked. Finally the group should share their own history of education and work so it can be compared to the others. The leader should summarize the findings looking for patterns and differences. Did education and/or work have any relationship to happiness?

Were they related to economics and/or class, to the number of generations in the U.S.? Did lack of education and/or opportunity to work cause a woman to encourage her daughter to get what the mother had missed or did she encourage her daughter to be like her?

3. Sweet Sixteen. This is a variation on the preceding exercise. Again the group should be divided into groups of 6 to 8 people. The participants should relax and close their eyes while the leader describes the situation:

> "You are visiting your grandmother when she is 16 years old. See how she looks, what she is wearing. You are very close. She is telling you about her dreams. What she hopes for the future. How she sees herself when she grows up. What she expects out of her life. What does she tell you?"

Each participant should have a chance to describe this to at least one other person. If time allows each member should share with the others. Then repeat the exercise for the mother, and finally for the woman herself.

The leader should help the group to examine the differences in the women's roles and expectations. This exercise is designed to help women understand how the dreams, achievements and disappointments of their grandmother may have influenced their own mother's dreams, and in that way influenced their own life. The age is 16 because that is a time when girls can dream about their future, but still have some realistic sense of what lies ahead in their life. It is a time of possibility and reality.

4. Dreams, Hopes and Disappointments. In groups of 6 to 8 have each member share the following information first for the grandmother then their mother:

> What was expected of her?
> What gave her pleasure?

What did she do to give pleasure to
others?
What was she most proud of?
What was her biggest disappointment?

After each woman has had a chance to share, have
them consider how they are like their grandmother
and/or mother, and how they are different. Can
they see the origins of these similarities and
differences?

5.   Changing Lives. In any of the preceding exercises
the following questions can be included:

In describing the grandmother and/or mother did
she assume the role she did because:

it was expected of her?
she was afraid to change?
to please her family?
of habit?
of lethargy to act?
of her own free will?
of personal ambition?
of other reasons? What reasons?

In such a discussion the leader should be trying
to gain insights into why some of the women were
so strong and self-sufficient, looking for the
positive role-models and factors which helped to
make them that way.

6.   Laughing at Ourselves. We each do things that are
totally irrational, but we do them anyway. For
some it is how we spend money that does not relate
to how much money we have. One example is the
woman who can afford to buy expensive clothes but
only shops at sales. Or the woman who cannot
stand to spend money on a meal in a restaurant,
although she will spend money freely on other
activities. We may be meticulously clean or
rebelliously sloppy. Some of these behaviors are
a direct reaction to something our parents either
did, or did not do. They may stem from childhood
statements such as "I'll never do that when I grow
up." They may grow from poverty, or our parent's
fear of poverty. They may grow from shame about
something our mothers did or did not do.

In groups of 6 to 8 have the members share these behaviors. This is usually very relaxed, because many of the things we share are very amusing. After the initial sharing each person should try to put this behavior into perspective, exploring the origin in themselves and how it relates to their mother. They may want to consider changing that particular behavior.

These exercises are all designed to give us a sense of the flow of our own history and our responses to it. They should help us consider the similarities and differences between ourselves and the women before us.

Conclusions

These exercises require a 3 x 5" card and pencil. Each member should do them alone before sharing with the whole circle. A moving closing is to have the women stand in a circle as they read their cards, then sing together with arms joined, or move slowly in the circle in a simple dance.

1. A Gift from the Past.

If your grandmother could give you a gift, what would it be?

If your mother could give you a gift, what would it be?

If you could give a gift to your grandmother what would it be?

If you could give a gift to your mother what would it be?

What gift would you like to give to yourself?

An alternative is to substitute one of the following words for the word "gift":

Value   Character   Trait

Another option is to have the women write the answers to the questions above, and if it is possible to have a fire, in a fireplace, campfire, barbecue or even in a large, safe fireproof bowl (make sure this is on a bed of sand or other

136

fireproof material), have the women step toward the fire, read their card and put it into the fire. This can be a very effective and moving closure.

2. ZAKOR. The leader should help the group to relax and give them the following directions: "Take an object that you brought to share. Close your eyes while you hold it and take a sense of its essence into your being. Now write on your card one word describing how it feels. Next write a word describing how it smells. Next write a word describing a sound connected to it. Then describe a taste connected with it. Finally how it looks."

    What has been created is a poem about the object. Let the participants share their creations in a random way--don't try going around the circle as some women may feel uncomfortable sharing in this way.*3

3. Naming. The women may want to choose new names for their grandmother, their mother and themselves that have a symbolic meaning to them.

    The final exercise should be simple. Once the leader has given the directions she should step back into the group to become one with them. The ending should flow from the exercise into movement and song, possible a final hug. No explanations should be necessary.

*This was adapted from an exercise developed by:

    1. Judy Silverberg
    2. Gerald Bubis
    2. Laura Wine Pastor

GLORIFIED, VILIFIED--OR SATISFIED:
JEWISH WOMEN IN LITERATURE

Sondra Henry and Emily Taitz
Mid-Island YM/YWHA

This course complements Henry and Taitz' course, "Queens, Courtesans and Commoners: A Rare View of History," which appeared in the first edition of the Guide. It is part of a continuum of courses on Jewish women offered under the larger title, "Contemporary Jewish Women's Institute." The series begins with the basic history course included in the "Queens" syllabus, then continues with "Life Cycle of the Jewish Woman," which is followed by a course entitled, "Images of Jewish Women."

Presented here is the eight-session portion of this course that focuses on Jewish Women in Literature. This course is followed by a final course in the series, "The many faces of Eve: Jewish women in different communities," which includes studies of Jews in China and Japan, the Arab world, South America, Ethiopia, Israel, South Africa, and the U.S.S.R.

* * *

Session I BED, BREAD AND CANDLES: How the Jewish woman was portrayed in literature before the 19th century.
> Shakespeare, The Merchant of Venice (Jessica)
> Walter Scott, Ivanhoe (Rebecca)
> George Eliot, Daniel Deronda

Session II THE IMMIGRANT EXPERIENCE: The immigrant woman confronted distinctive problems in assimilating to the American way of life.
> Mary Antin, The Promised Land, N.Y.: Houghton Mifflin, 1969
> Anzia Yezierska, Bread Givers, N.Y.: Braziller, 1975 (PB) N.Y.: Persea Books, 1975
> The Open Cage, N.Y.: Persea Books, 1979 (PB)
> Kramer and Masur, (eds.), Jewish Grandmothers, (Boston, Beacon, 1976)

Session III	THE DEPRESSION AND THE 1930'S: The Jewish mother was idealized in novels of this period. An analysis of these portrayals in two novels against the background of the period.

Session III — THE DEPRESSION AND THE 1930'S: The Jewish mother was idealized in novels of this period. An analysis of these portrayals in two novels against the background of the period.

Henry Roth, Call It Sleep, (N.Y., 1935, reprint Avon Books)

Sholem Asch, The Mother, (N.Y., 1930, reprint 1970)

Nathan Glazer, American Judaism

Session IV — WORLD WAR II AND ITS AFTERMATH: The Jewish woman before, during and after the Holocaust.

Susan Schaeffer, Anya, (N.Y., Avon Books, 1976)

Herman Wouk, Marjorie Morningstar, (N.Y., 1955, Pocket Books, 1973, PB)

Ruth Gruber, Raquela, Woman of Israel

Session V — AFFLUENCE AND INFLUENCE: Upward Mobility and movement to the suburbs.

Philip Roth, Goodbye Columbus, (Meridian, Cleveland, 1962)

Portnoy's Complaint, (N.Y., Random House, 1967)

Session VI — EXOTIC AND EROTIC VIEWS OF JEWISH WOMEN

Singer, I.B., Shosha, (N.Y., Fawcett, 1978)

Enemies, A Love Story; "Zeitl & Rickel" in The Seance

Agnon, S.Y., The Lady and the Peddlar

Session VII — WOMEN'S LIBERATION: Is it good for Jewish Women?

Erica Jong, Fear of Flying, (N.Y., Signet, 1973)

Gail Parent, Sheila Levine is Dead and Living in New York, (N.Y., Putnam's Sons, 1972)

Session VIII — WHITHER JEWISH FEMINISM: Future or Fiasco?

Nina Schneider, The Woman Who Lived in a Prologue, (N.Y., Houghton Mifflin, 1979)

SESSION VIII   Betty Friedan, The Feminine
(cont.)   Mystique; It Changed My Life; The
                         Second Stage, (N.Y., Summit,
                         1982)

CONTRIBUTORS

EVELYN TORTON BECK directs the program in Women's Studies at the University of Maryland. Previously on the faculty of the University of Wisconsin at Madison, she is author of **Kafka and the Jewish Theatre**, co-author of **The Prism of Sex: Essays in the Sociology of Knowledge** and editor of **Nice Jewish Girls: A Lesbian Anthology**. She received her Ph.D. from the University of Wisconsin.

DEBORAH BUDNER is a 1986 graduate of Oberlin College. While at Oberlin, she was a co-creator of "A Woman's Haggadah" by Miriam's Timbrel, and developed and taught "Children of Sarah," which appears here. She continues to explore the intersection of Jewish studies and women's studies.

SUE LEVI ELWELL serves as rabbi of Leo Baeck Temple in Los Angeles. She is the co-author, with Edward Levenson, of the first edition of the **Jewish Women's Studies Guide**, of **Jewish Women: A Mini-Course for Jewish Schools**, and co-editor, with Drorah Setel, of **The Jewish Calendar 5746**. She earned an M.S. and Ph.D. from Indiana University and an M.A.H.L. and rabbinic ordination from Hebrew Union College-Jewish Institute of Religion.

IRENE FINE is the Founder and Director of the Women's Institute for Continuing Jewish Education in San Diego. At the Institute she teaches courses in Jewish history and on writing midrash and developing new ceremonies and rituals. She is the author of **Midlife and Its Rite of Passage Ceremony** and **Educating the New Jewish Woman: A Dynamic Approach.** Currently she is at work on a new text: **The Ceremony of the Wise Woman: A Celebration for Elders.** She received her Ph.D. from the Union for Experimenting Colleges and Universities.

SONDRA HENRY is co-author, with Emily Taitz, of **Written Out of History: Our Jewish Foremothers.** Together they have taught and lectured widely in Jewish women's studies. Henry, a graduate of Bennington College, holds a J.D. from Columbia Law School, and is a practicing attorney.

PAULA E. HYMAN is the Lucy G. Moses Professor of Modern Jewish History at Yale University. She received bachelor's degrees from Radcliffe College and the Hebrew College of Boston and her M.A. and Ph.D. degrees from Columbia University. She is a co-author of **The Jewish Woman in America** and author of **From Dreyfus to Vichy: the Remaking of French Jewry: 1906-1939.** Most recently, she has co-edited a volume entitled **The Jewish Family: Myths and Reality.**

SHARON KLEINBAUM, formerly assistant director of the National Yiddish Book Center in Amherst, Massachusetts, is pursuing rabbinical studies at the Reconstructionist Rabbinical College in Philadelphia. She is a graduate of Barnard College.

EDWARD R. ZWEIBACK LEVENSON is Assistant Principal of Kerem Torah School, Vineland, N.J. He co-edited the first edition of the **Jewish Women's Studies Guide** (with Sue Levi Elwell), and is the author of articles on Jewish history and Jewish women's studies. He received his Ph.D. from Brandeis University, and has taught at the University of Wisconsin, Gratz College, and Villanova University.

RELA GEFFEN MONSON is Professor of Sociology and chair of the faculty at Gratz College in Philadelphia. She is the author of **Academy and Community: A Study of the Jewish Identity and Involvement of Professors, Bringing Women In: A Survey of the Evolving Role of Women in Jewish Organizational Life,** and articles on the American Jewish community and the changing Jewish family. She is a graduate of the Joint Program of Columbia University and the Teacher's Institute of the Jewish Theological Seminary, and earned her Ph.D. from the University of Florida.

MIRIAM PESKOWITZ, co-creator with Deborah Budner of "Children of Sarah," is also a 1986 graduate of Oberlin College. While a student at Oberlin, she learned how to combine her academic interests with a range of spiritual experiences and political activism. She looks forward to graduate studies that will explore the issues of power and gender in Hellenistic Judaism and intertestamental literature.

FAITH ROGOW, a graduate of Indiana University, is a Ph.D. candidate in Women's History at State University of New York at Binghamton. She is currently writing her dissertation on the history of the National Council of Jewish Women.

MAXINE SCHWARTZ SELLER is professor in the Graduate School of Education and Adjunct Professor in the Department of History at the State University of New York at Buffalo. Her publications include **To Seek America: A History of Ethnic Life in the United States, Immigrant Women, Ethnic Theatre in the United States,** and many articles and book chapters on the history and education of immigrants and women in the United States. She received her B.A. from Bryn Mawr College and her M.A. and Ph.D. from the University of Pennsylvania.

T. DRORAH SETEL is the author of numerous articles on women in Judaism, co-editor of the **Jewish Calendar 5746,** and is currently at work on her first book, **Making Our Own Way: Feminist Paths in Judaism,** to be published in the fall of 1988. She received her B.A. from Swarthmore College, her M.T.S. from Harvard Divinity School and studied in the rabbinic program at Leo Baeck College, London.

MARCIA COHN SPIEGEL, who earned an M.A. in Jewish Communal Service from Hebrew Union College-Jewish Institute of Religion, teaches continuing education courses in women's studies at the University of Judaism and in synagogues and community centers throughout Southern California. She is the author of **Women in the Bible: A Study Guide, The Jewish Woman: A Portrait in her Own Words, The Heritage of Noah: Alcoholism in the Jewish Community Today,** and co-author of the forthcoming **Women Speak to God: The Poems and Prayers of Jewish Women through the Ages.**

EMILY TAITZ, co-author with Sondra Henry of **Written Out of History: Our Jewish Fore-mothers,** is a Ph.D. candidate in Medieval Jewish History at the Jewish Theological Seminary of America. She holds a B.A. from Queens College and an M.A. from J.T.S. She has published, taught and lectured on Jewish women's issues. She and Sondra Henry are also the authors of a biography of Gloria Steinem for young readers that will be published Spring, 1987.

CELIA Y. WEISMAN, until recently, the Director of the NYC Jewish Women's Resource Center, has taught women's studies and religious studies at Barnard College and New York University, and lectured on Jewish women in the New York area. A summa cum laude Phi Beta Kappa graduate of Barnard College, Ms. Weisman holds an MA in Comparative Religion from Columbia University.

MARGARET MOERS WENIG, rabbi of Beth Am, the People's Temple in New York, is Instructor of Liturgy and Philosophy/Theology at the School of Sacred Music and the Rabbinic School of Hebrew Union College-Jewish Institute of Religion. She is the co-author of **Siddur Nashim: A Sabbath Prayerbook for Women,** and of articles on rabbinic literature. She is a graduate of Brown University, and received her M.A.H.L. and rabbinic ordination from Hebrew Union College-Jewish Institute of Religion.